PRAISE FOR
JESUS IS THE QUESTION

"Some say that Jesus is the answer to all of our questions. They may be right. But before that is the case, Jesus is something different. He is the one who asks the questions—hundreds of them, it turns out. In this marvelous collection of reflections, Martin Copenhaver helps readers to deeply hear the questions Jesus asks of us. In doing so he challenges a church that too easily adapts Jesus to North American culture's penchant for quick fixes and easy answers. In truth, Jesus is not so much the solution for our problems as he is the problem for our solutions."

—Anthony B. Robinson, teacher and author of
Changing the Conversation: A Third Way for Congregations

"Language, all language, at its very core is relational—one person entering into a relationship with another. If that doesn't happen, more often than not we are diminished in soul. Jesus, the 'Word made flesh,' was a master at drawing those around him into relationship. Martin Copenhaver demonstrates how he does this by using questions, a lot of them. Take these questions seriously and let them draw you more deeply into the company of Jesus."

—Eugene Peterson, Professor Emeritus of Spiritual Theology,
Regent College, Vancouver, B.C.,
and author of *The Message* translation of the Bible

"As someone who lives in the land of *Jesus Is the Answer*, I deeply appreciate the way this book restores the ministry of the question, all 307 of them. With his typical eloquence and pastoral voice, Copenhaver makes a compelling case for faith as a journey, not a destination. Take and read.

When you spend your life as a pastor, you live the questions in covenant with the people you love. Martin Copenhaver has done a wise and wonderful thing in this book. He reminds us that faith begins when we are invited into conversation—with ourselves, with one another, and with God. *Jesus Is the Question* should be required reading in the Beloved Community."

—Rev. Dr. Robin R. Meyers, senior minister of Mayflower Congregational
UCC Church of Oklahoma City and Distinguished Professor of Social
Justice at Oklahoma City University, author of *The Underground Church:
Reclaiming the Subversive Way of Jesus*

"This outstanding book is what thoughtful Jesus followers have been waiting for—a reminder that our questions matter. Welcome to the early world of Jesus. Like many people today, they thought they wanted answers, and simple ones at that. Instead, they got so much more.

By showing us all the questions Jesus asks, Copenhaver has come up with a classic. Get ready for some exciting conversation and some serious insight.

WARNING: This book could lead to more questions. That's a good thing!"

—Lillian Daniel, senior minister of First Congregational Church, UCC, in Glen Ellyn, IL, and author of When "Spiritual But Not Religious" Is Not Enough

"Martin Copenhaver is a pastor, a scholar, an adept communicator of the Christian faith, and a leader in theological education. One reason why Martin is such a good preacher is that he has the ability to ask good questions: Why do we do church the way we do? Why are our attempts to communicate the Christian faith not as interesting as Jesus? What's ahead in our attempt to be faithful to God in Christ? I now know that Martin got his ability to ask provocative questions from Jesus. In this wonderful book, Jesus stands before us as a provocateur who rattles our cages through penetrating questions. Both Christians who think they have all the answers and Christians who are mired in unanswerable questions will love reading this book."

—William Willimon, United Methodist Bishop, retired, Professor of the Practice of Christian Ministry, Duke Divinity School, and Pastor, Duke Memorial United Methodist Church, Durham, NC

"Only a seasoned pastor could have written this book. Martin Copenhaver draws from his profound years in parish ministry to illustrate that more is found in questions than in answers—especially when Jesus is the one asking the questions. This is a great book for small groups to study together."

—M. Craig Barnes, President, Princeton Theological Seminary

"According to John's Gospel, people came to a follower of Jesus and begged, 'Sir, we would like to see Jesus.' In this compelling book, Martin Copenhaver helps the reader to do just that—to see Jesus from a fresh perspective. The Jesus who emerges in these pages does not dole out pat answers to life's hard questions. Rather, Jesus asks provocative questions to evoke new understandings and change lives."

—Frederick Buechner

JESUS is the QUESTION

THE 307 QUESTIONS JESUS ASKED AND THE 3 HE ANSWERED

MARTIN B. COPENHAVER

Abingdon Press

Nashville

JESUS IS THE QUESTION
THE 307 QUESTIONS JESUS ASKED
AND THE 3 HE ANSWERED

Library of Congress Cataloging-in-Publication Data

Copenhaver, Martin B., 1954-
    Jesus is the question : the 307 questions Jesus asked and the 3 He answered / Martin B. Copenhaver.
        pages cm
    ISBN 978-1-4267-5514-9 (binding: soft back, trade, pbk. : alk. paper)   1. Jesus Christ—Miscellanea.   2. Questioning.   3. Jesus Christ—Teachings.   I. Title.
    BS2415.C65 2014
    232.9'54—dc23

2014008261

The majority of scripture is taken from the Common English Bible. Copyright © 2011 by the Common English Bible. All rights reserved. Used by permission. www.CommonEnglishBible.com.

Matthew 6:28-30 on page 136 is taken from The Holy Bible, English Standard Version® (ESV®), copyright © 2001 by Crossway, a publishing ministry of Good News Publishers. Used by permission. All rights reserved.

Mark 8:15 on page 85 is taken from the Holy Bible: International Standard Version®. Copyright © 2003 by The ISV Foundation. Used by permission of Davidson Press, Inc. ALL RIGHTS RESERVED INTERNATIONALLY.

Scripture taken from the New Revised Standard Version of the Bible, copyright 1989, Division of Christian Education of the National Council of the Churches of Christ in the United States of America. Used by permission. All rights reserved.

14 15 16 17 18 19 20 21 22 23—10 9 8 7 6 5 4 3 2 1

MANUFACTURED IN THE UNITED STATES OF AMERICA

For Kathy Musser,
Beloved colleague in ministry at Village Church
for seventeen years

"What is the answer?" she asked, and when no answer came she laughed and then said, "Then, what is the question?"

—Gertrude Stein's last words

CONTENTS

FOREWORD

Lauren F. Winner

I SERVE A CHURCH IN A SMALL TOWN in Piedmont, North Carolina. The town has a college, and the college has a labyrinth, designed by one of my parishioners.

I have known for some years that one of the ways you can pray in a labyrinth is to approach the labyrinth with a question. So if there is something in your life you are trying to discern or decide—if, to borrow from the poet Marie Howe, you are asking yourself, "Should I take the job? Move to the city? Should I try to conceive a child in my middle age?"— you might hold that question in mind and ask it of yourself and God as you move through the labyrinth.

What I didn't realize, until I read the wonderful book you now hold in your hands, is that our questions don't always come from us. Sometimes they come from God. (Indeed, I didn't realize, until I read this book, that one of Jesus' favorite modes of communication is to ask a question. I didn't know that according to the Gospels, Jesus asks 307 different questions, is asked only 183 questions, and answers fewer than 10 of those he is asked. Amazing!)

Over the last few weeks, I have approached the labyrinth with a question—one of the questions Jesus asks:

> What are you looking for?
>
> Why would people gain the whole world but lose their lives?
>
> Do you love me?
>
> Where is your faith?

※ ※ ※ ※

What does it mean that Jesus asks so many questions? I don't think it means that Jesus is vague or ambivalent. I don't think it means that Jesus is wishy-washy. I think Jesus' questions mean something else altogether.

Linguists tell us that questions have many different functions in conversation:

> Questions elicit information.
>
> Questions inspire people to discover something new, to unearth new knowledge.
>
> Questions also persuade: this is how hotshot courtroom attorneys win their cases. They ask questions of a witness, but those questions make an argument, and ultimately the chain of questions persuades the jury.

Questions stimulate thought. That's why good
teachers ask questions of their students rather
than just lecture at them.

And questions forge intimacy. That's why you sometimes leave a conversation in which many questions have been exchanged feeling noticeably connected to the person with whom you were speaking. (Imagine here not an interrogation, but the questions you exchange over coffee with a new friend.) We feel that sense of connection because the questions have bespoken (or sparked) mutual curiosity. The questions have created a sense of collaboration. We have asked questions of one another because we share some interest—or because we are interested in one another. The questions, in turn, deepen that shared interest. So questions build closeness. Maybe this is one reason Jesus is always asking questions: it is one way to create intimacy between him and us.

❦ ❦ ❦ ❦

But, oh, how Jesus' questions also disarm.

Consider just the first question this book investigates: Jesus' asking his disciples (and then later his arresters, and then later still Mary, at the empty tomb), "What are you looking for?"

I find this a disconcerting question—so disconcerting that my tendency is to bat it away rather than really hear it.

What am I looking for? I am not really sure.

If you look at how I actually spend my hours—and surely how we use our time is probably a pretty good index of what we are looking for—you might say that I am looking for professional identity or financial security. These are not, I hasten to add, inherently bad things. They are just not the ultimate things, and when Jesus next drops by and asks me what I'm looking for, I don't really want to say "financial security."

Another way to discover what you are really looking for is to ask the people closest to you. If their answers seem congruent with your own sense of things, it will be a pleasing conversation. But be forewarned—you might not like their answers at all. I asked my husband what he thinks I am looking for, and he said intellectually stimulating conversation partners and intensity. I suppose Michael's answer could have been worse. He could have said I was looking for bonbons or meanness. But frankly, his answer seems kind of lame and disappointing, and I am not at all sure I want to be a person whose greatest longing is an intellectually stimulating chat.

And so I took the question to the labyrinth. And there I heard what I would like the answer to be: "I am looking for my true self; I am looking for a genuine encounter with my neighbor; I am looking for God—sometimes I look in my neighbors' faces for God, sometimes I look on hilltops or sometimes under couch cushions, sometimes I look in the bread and wine." In the labyrinth, I heard that there is a way in which this is a true answer for me. And then there is a way in which it is only an ideal: if I were the person I would like to be, I would be looking for true encounter with God, neighbor, and self; but in reality I am looking for an intense discussion about eighteenth-century agricultural policy and some good advice about Roth IRAs.

❦ ❦ ❦

It is now several days after I walked the labyrinth, several days after Jesus' piercing question about my longing, and I am beginning to rethink the dichotomy between intimacy and uneasiness, between a question's capacity to draw me closer to Jesus and a question's capacity to unnerve me. I think I feel a closeness between me and my true self, and a closeness between me and God, being quickened right there in the place that Jesus' question rankles. Right there in the place where the question unsettles, I feel some new intimacy sparked.

It is the intimacy of hearing a true question and of being willing to entertain hazarding a true answer.

I want to take each and every question this book poses—which is to say, each and every question Jesus poses—into the labyrinth, into prayer, into my conversations with God, and into my conversations with myself. In that way, *Jesus Is the Question* is becoming a staple of my spiritual life, and I hope it might become a staple of your spiritual life, too. I am almost envious of what you will hear, what you will discover, in these questions, in this book.

INTRODUCTION

SO MANY QUESTIONS

❖❖❖❖❖❖❖❖❖

I HAVE BEEN HANGING OUT WITH JESUS for a long time. I have been a Christian all my life, and I have been an ordained minister for as many years as Jesus lived (for those keeping score at home, that's thirty-three years). I heard the Gospel stories before I was old enough to read, and by now I have read the Gospels more times than I can count. I have led Bible studies on every recorded nook of Jesus' life and preached on every cranny of his teachings.

Of course, even after all this time, I continue to learn new things from Jesus and about him. One of the alluring things about Jesus is there is always more to learn. With each reading there are new insights and overlooked details that keep the stories about Jesus fresh no matter how many times you read them.

But I confess I didn't think I could still learn something about Jesus that would fundamentally transform my view of him.

That changed when a friend said, "Have you noticed that

in the Gospels Jesus asks a ton of questions? In every situation, he's asking questions. I think Jesus may have asked even more questions than Socrates ever did."

I found his observation intriguing, and it left me eager to learn more. I set out on a quest for the questioning Jesus, not knowing at the time that the journey would lead to something like hidden treasure, a transformative new understanding: asking questions is central to Jesus' life and teachings. Jesus is a questioner. Jesus is not the ultimate Answer Man—he's more like the Great Questioner.

Jesus asks many more questions than he is asked. In the four Gospels Jesus asks 307 different questions. By contrast, he is only asked 183 questions.

More striking still, Jesus directly answers very few of the 183 questions he is asked. Two published studies state that Jesus directly answers only 3 of the 183 questions he is asked.[1] According to my count, Jesus directly answers as many as 8 of the questions he is asked, but whichever count you go with, it is an astonishingly small number. (Although the focus of this book is on the questions Jesus asks, a chapter is devoted to the questions Jesus answers directly.)

Jesus prefers to ask questions rather than to provide direct answers. Jesus chooses to ask a question 307 times in the Gospel accounts. Even if Jesus gives direct answers to as many as 8 ques-

♦♦♦♦♦♦♦♦♦

"Have you noticed that in the Gospels Jesus asks a ton of questions? In every situation, he's asking questions. I think Jesus may have asked even more questions than Socrates ever did."

tions, that still means that Jesus is almost 40 times more likely to ask a question than he is to give a direct answer.

It is telling that the first words Jesus speaks in the Gospels are in the form of a question. According to Luke, Mary and Joseph lose track of their twelve-year-old son Jesus in the Temple in Jerusalem. They are frantic with worry. When they finally track down Jesus, they find him "sitting among the teachers, listening to them and"—note this—"putting questions to them." When his parents express their dismay for being caused such anxiety, the preteen Jesus responds by asking two questions: "Why were you looking for me? Didn't you know that it was necessary for me to be in my Father's house?"

At the other end of Jesus' life, according to Mark and Matthew, his last utterance, while on the cross, was yet another question: "My God, my God, why have you forsaken me?" (Matthew 27:46; Mark 15:34).

We might assume that, if ever there were a time when Jesus would stick to simple, declarative sentences, it would be after his resurrection. According to the Gospels, however, even the risen Christ keeps asking questions:

> "What are you talking about as you walk
> along?"

> "Do you have anything here to eat?"

> "Do you love me?"

In a conversation with two friends I shared my interest in the questions Jesus asks. Both readily embraced the notion of a Questioning Jesus. As the conversation proceeded, however, it became clear that they were responding eagerly for different reasons. One friend said, "I love the idea that Jesus has so many questions because so do I. That's a comfort." The other friend then said, "Funny, knowing that Jesus asks a lot of questions does not sound comforting to me. It sounds decidedly disquieting because I assume Jesus will use questions to challenge me."

And, of course, both of my friends are right, as will become clear when we delve into the particular questions Jesus asks in the chapters that follow.

Jesus asks different kinds of questions in the Gospels, and to different ends. Some seem simple and straightforward ("What are you talking about as you walk along?"). Other questions are rhetorical. They are meant to hang in the air unanswered ("Who among you by worrying can add a single moment to your life?").

Other questions that Jesus asks probe the depths and elude any easy answer:

"What are you looking for?"

"But who do you say that I am?"

Still other questions are a direct challenge to the listener:

"Why do you not understand what I am saying?"

"Where is your faith?"

"Why could you not watch with me one hour?"

Jesus asks some questions that seem silly, at least at first reading. When Peter tries walking on water and eventually begins to sink, Jesus asks him, "You man of weak faith! Why did you begin to have doubts?" Why did Peter begin to doubt? Because he was walking on water, that's why. That sounds like a silly question to me. Or is it?

✦✦✦✦✦✦✦✦✦

We hear the affirmation in gospel songs and read it on bumper stickers: "Jesus is the answer." But might Jesus also be the question?

When a blind man cries out to Jesus as he passes by on the road to Jericho, Jesus responds by asking him, "What do you want me to do for you?"

Is that another silly question? If you are blind, of course what you want is to have your sight restored. Does Jesus have to ask? Actually, it seems to be one of Jesus' favorite questions because he repeats it in other similar circumstances. Most of us have a tendency to assume we know what another person needs or wants. By asking the blind man, "What do you want me to do for you?" Jesus is showing respect for him. He is not presuming to know what he wants. He is asking.

According to John's Gospel, there is another question Jesus asks repeatedly and in a variety of circumstances. Jesus asks it at the beginning of his ministry when people begin to follow him: "What are you looking for?" Twice he asks a variation of that question of those who are about to arrest him: "Who are you looking for?" He asks it again of the women who gather at the empty tomb: "Who are you looking for?" It is the kind of question that is worth repeating over time and in various circumstances because it can sound different and can elicit different answers each time.

"Who are you looking for?" The premise of this book is that if we are looking for an Answer Man Jesus, it is likely we will be disappointed, but there is great value in pondering the implications of having a savior who approaches the world—and us—with questions.

Contrary to how Jesus often is portrayed, he does not offer spiritual tips. He does not give us a neat list of ten ways we can be closer to God. He does not provide easy answers. Instead, he asks hard questions. In that he is like the Zen master who asks questions to take us beyond the obvious to something deeper. He is like Socrates, who taught the people simply by asking probing questions. He is like the prophets, who railed against the ruling authorities and sought justice by asking challenging questions.

One of the older members of the first church I served, who was a person of great faith, would comment on the mysteries of life by saying, "When I meet Jesus, I will have a lot of questions for him." But might Jesus also have a lot of questions for her?

A friend tells of being in the class of a legendary professor of theology who completed his final lecture to a standing ovation. The professor picked up his notes, hastened them into a folder, and headed out of the lecture hall. At the doorway he turned around and faced the applauding students. The class fell silent, listening for a parting word. The professor took in the class with his eyes and said, "Just remember: Jesus is the question to all of your answers." And, with that, he left.

Catholic author Richard Rohr writes, "In general, we can see that Jesus' style is almost exactly the opposite of modern televangelism or even the mainline church approach of 'Dear

Abby' bits of inspiring advice and workable solutions for daily living. Jesus is too much the Jewish prophet to merely stabilize the status quo with platitudes."[2]

Easy answers can give us a sense of finality. By entertaining questions God has a chance to change us. Answers can be offered as a conclusion. Questions are an invitation to further reflection. For the most part, answers close and questions open. It is telling that the word *question* contains the word *quest.* That is, a question sends you on a journey and often in search of something valuable.

The questions Jesus asks have a lot in common with another of his favorite teaching tools—parables. In both question and parable, Jesus is able to communicate indirectly. In both, the listener has to do some of the work. If the goal is to communicate a body of knowledge, then the direct communication of a lecture is appropriate. But the goal of both question and parable is different. The goal is not to communicate knowledge but to elicit new understanding in the listener. Information is not the goal. Transformation is.

There are considerable rewards in spending time with the questions Jesus asks. Some of those questions have a way of taking us deeper in a way that simple answers are unable to do. That may be one reason why the poet Rainer Maria Rilke offered this famous advice to a young poet: "Live the questions now. Perhaps then, someday in the future, you will gradually, without even noticing it, live your way into the answer."[3]

I had a hunch that, in asking so many questions, Jesus was reflecting a Jewish tradition, perhaps particularly a rabbinic tradition. (In fact, there is an old Jewish joke about the proclivity to ask questions: "Why does a Jew always answer a question with a question?" Answer: "Why shouldn't a Jew always answer a question with a question?") I have no expertise in this area, however, so I met with Rabbi Daniel Lehmann, a rabbinic scholar and President of Hebrew College, to learn something about the role of asking questions in Jewish tradition.

Rabbi Lehmann reminded me that the Passover Seder, the paradigmatic ritual of Jewish tradition, is structured around questions. The Seder is a ritual feast that marks the beginning of Passover. Central to the Seder is a retelling of the story of the liberation of the Israelites from slavery in ancient Egypt. The retelling of the story is prompted by the asking of five questions, beginning with, "Why is this night different from all other nights?" These questions are a teaching tool, so it is customary that they are asked by the youngest child at the table. The ritual then moves to questions about the Seder asked by "four sons"—one who is wise, one who is wicked, one who is simple, and one who does not know how to ask. The ability to ask questions is so valued that the son "who does not know how to ask" is mentioned last, even after the one who is called "simple."

The Talmud, a central text of Judaism, also is structured around questions. The Talmud is a record of rabbinic discussions pertaining to Jewish law, ethics, customs, and history—hundreds of pages of rabbinic debates, sparked by questions that require the rabbis' discernment and wisdom. The oldest portions of the Talmud date back to 200 CE, however, which means they were written more than a hundred years after the

Gospels. But can the questions Jesus asked be read in the context of this rabbinic tradition?

Some of the questions asked in the Talmud seem, at first blush, narrower than the questions Jesus asked—very precise questions about dietary codes, property disputes, and the correct time for prayer. Yet in the context of the Talmud, those questions are ultimately questions about life and meaning, about how individuals and communities can best live with one another and God—not entirely unlike the questions Jesus asked. In the Gospels, Jesus is addressed as Rabbi because he is, among other things, a teacher. And a good rabbi knows how to ask questions.

The pages of this book are an occasion to linger with some of the questions Jesus asks. In the chapters that follow, we will reflect on particular questions. At the end of this book is a compilation of many of the questions Jesus asks. At any point you may want to dive into that vast sea of questions, a full immersion experience like none other.

So many questions.

Why does Jesus ask so many questions?

CHAPTER 1

QUESTIONS ABOUT LONGING

✦✦✦✦✦✦✦✦✦

IT IS ONE OF THE FEW QUESTIONS Jesus repeats. According to John's Gospel, Jesus asks this question repeatedly and in a variety of circumstances. John obviously thinks it is a key question because, in his narrative, Jesus asks it at such singular moments in his life. He asks it at the beginning of his ministry when people begin to follow him: "What are you looking for?" When a detachment of soldiers come to arrest him, Jesus twice asks a variation of that same question: "Who are you looking for?" Then, Jesus asks it again of the women who gather at the empty tomb: "Who are you looking for?" Obviously, Jesus thinks this is a question worth repeating, as if in some way it is *the* question.

"What are you looking for?" That question can be either straightforward or profound. It all depends on the context and who is asking the question. If you are gazing at a rack of suits in a clothing store and an employee of that store asks, "What are you looking for?" it's a rather simple question. But if the savior of the world asks, "What are you looking for?" that is another matter entirely. That question coming from that source is enough to make you pause and ponder.

"Who are you looking for?" Is that a straightforward question or a profound one? Once again, it all depends. If you are wandering the halls of an office, obviously lost, and someone asks, "Who are you looking for?" it's hardly a profound question. But when Jesus encounters his followers after the resurrection and asks the same question—"Who are you looking for?"—it's not nearly as straightforward or as easily answered.

In their current form and context, these questions Jesus asks are open-ended rather than closed-ended. There is a big difference.

A closed-ended question often implies an answer. For instance, if a loved one comes home from a shopping trip and asks, "How do I look in this outfit?" it would be a grave mistake to assume that is an open-ended question. After all, there is only one acceptable answer.

It is harder to ask open-ended questions than we might assume. It is more common for us to ask questions in a way that steers someone toward the answer we are looking for. For instance, if a member of your family has had a severe cold and you ask, "How do you feel today?" that is an open-ended question. But if you pose the question in a slightly different way, "Are you feeling better today?" that is no longer an open-ended question because it implies a preferred response. Either you are sympathetic enough to want the family member to feel better, or you are simply tired of hearing all of the complaints about being sick. Whatever the motivation, the question implies a desired response. By the way you ask the question, it is clear you want to hear that your family member is feeling better.

By contrast, an open-ended question does not seek to limit the responses. The answer to an open-ended question is not obvious or implied. For this reason, an open-ended question can expand our thinking. The answer to an open-ended question, such as those Jesus asks, can also change over time, so it helps to keep such a question continually before you.

Wayne Cordeiro shares this anecdote:

> An old story tells of a rabbi living in a Russian city a century ago. Disappointed by his lack of direction and life purpose, he wandered in the chilly evening. With his hands thrust deep in his pockets, he aimlessly walked through the empty streets, questioning his faith in God, the Scriptures and his calling to ministry. The only thing colder than the Russian winter air was the chill within his soul. He felt so enshrouded by his own despair that he mistakenly wandered into a Russian military compound off limits to civilians.
>
> The bark of a Russian soldier shattered the silence of the evening chill. "Who are you? And what are you doing here?"
>
> "Excuse me?" replied the rabbi.
>
> "I said, 'Who are you and what are you doing here?'"
>
> After a brief moment, the rabbi, in a

gracious tone so as not to provoke the soldier, said, "How much do you get paid every day?"

"What does that have to do with you?" the soldier retorted.

With the delight of someone making a new discovery, the rabbi said, "I will pay you the equal sum if you will ask me those same two questions every day: 'Who are you?' and 'What are you doing here?'"

The soldier in the story did not intend to ask open-ended questions, but the rabbi heard them—or chose to hear them—as open-ended. To the rabbi, they were profound questions about his identity as a person and the purpose of his life. Such open-ended questions are not easily answered and, thus, are worthy of further—even daily—reflection.[4]

It can be helpful to have such open-ended questions before us on an ongoing basis. And, incidentally, the point of the story would be largely the same if the questions the rabbi asked to hear every day were the questions Jesus asked: What are you looking for? Who are you looking for? Both pairs of open-ended questions can lead us to consider the ultimate end and purpose of our lives.

Open-ended questions are particularly helpful in putting us in touch with our deepest desires. In his book *Let Your Life Speak*, Parker Palmer tells about the Quaker practice of what is called a "clearness committee." Quite simply, that is a group that comes together to help an individual gain clarity ("clearness") about something of importance to him or her. The members of the group do not give advice but merely ask probing, open-ended questions. Palmer tells of the time he was offered the presidency of a small college, which represented a very different vocational direction in his life. So Palmer, a lifelong Quaker, sat with a clearness committee.

They began by asking open-ended questions related to Palmer's vision for the school's mission in the larger society. Then someone asked, "What would you like most about being the president?" Palmer responded, "Well, I would not like having to give up my writing and my teaching....I would not like the politics of the presidency....I would not like having to glad-hand people I do not respect....I would not like..."

The person who posed the original question interrupted Palmer: "May I remind you that I asked what you would most *like*?"

Palmer responded, "Yes, yes, I'm working my way toward an answer. I would not like having to give up my summer vacations....I would not like having to wear a suit and tie all of the time....I would not like..."

Once again the questioner called him back to the original question. "Well," said Palmer in a small voice, "I guess what I'd like most is getting my picture in the paper with the word *president* under it." There was a long Quaker silence. The questioner had one more question: "Parker, can you think of an easier way to get your picture in the paper?"[5]

Of course, this last question is not open-ended, but it was made possible by the clarity that came from the open-ended questions that preceded it.

What are you looking for? Who are you looking for? Those are questions that can stick with us our whole lives long, and largely because they are not so easily answered.

What are you looking for, anyway? We don't always know. And that can be disquieting. In U2's hit song "I Still Haven't Found What I'm Looking For," lead singer Bono sings of a range of human experiences, both the highs and lows of life, but he always comes back to the refrain: "But I still haven't found what I'm looking for." The song is up-tempo, but Bono sings the refrain in a voice that expresses anguish, which is fitting. It can be difficult not to find what you are looking for. The song implies something more, however. As the refrain is repeated throughout the song, it becomes evident that the singer doesn't know what he is looking for—and that is more challenging still.

You pad into the kitchen, go directly to the refrigerator, open the door, and peer in. You are vaguely hungry, but you cannot tell exactly what you are hungry for. You survey the options. Cheese? No, that's not it. Cold sausage pizza? No, definitely not. Leftover salad? That's not quite it. You go so far as to take a bite of strawberry yogurt but put it back on the shelf.

The refrigerator is full enough, and your stomach is empty enough, but nothing seems exactly right. The cold air emerges and brings with it the remembered voice of your mother: "Don't leave the refrigerator door open." So you close the door and wait for the cold air to dissipate and the voice to fade. Then you open the refrigerator again, lean on the door, and stare blankly at the options, hoping that one will finally beckon and fully satisfy.

✦✦✦✦✦✦✦✦✦

What are you looking for? Who are you looking for? Those are questions that can stick with us our whole lives long, and largely because they are not so easily answered.

Many of us spend our lives like that, with indistinct long-ings we don't know how to satisfy. We yearn for something and know not what. We try a bit of this and that, for a time, or perhaps only in our imaginations, but nothing is quite right or enough to satisfy. You can never get enough of that which does not satisfy. So often we don't know what we want and then are disappointed when we don't get it.

A television news report told the story of a group of men who spent years in the pursuit of a particular stash of treasure they knew was buried off the coast of Florida. One day they uncovered it; and it was everything they had hoped and imag-ined it would be—golden coins and priceless antique jewelry. Success at last. Of course, there was great jubilation at the discovery, but there was also a hint of something else. The report ended with a picture of one of the discoverers, looking at nothing in particular with an almost wistful expression. And while that picture was on the screen, the reporter closed by asking this question and letting it dangle in the air: "What do you do when you have found what you were looking for?"

Oscar Wilde may be right: "There are two tragedies in life. One is to lose your heart's desire. The other is to gain it."

In an article entitled "Loved, but Abandoned and Sold," the *New York Times* reported on an auction of the contents of 960 abandoned safe-deposit boxes.[6] In most cases the rent on the safe-deposit boxes had not been paid for years, and every attempt had been made to return the contents to the owners. When the banks discovered that the owner of a box had died, the items were turned over to that person's estate. So most of the safe-deposit boxes in the auction were owned and aban-doned by people who were still alive. They just didn't want the stuff anymore. There was sterling silver flatware, antique coins, several gold watches, a pair of diamond earrings, and an engagement ring. And then there were items of sentimental value that were not included in the auction but merely discarded: old love letters and photographs, children's drawings, diplomas, and military citations.

Whether or not the items would command money at an auction, they represent the accomplishments and the longings in the lives of these people. They are the treasures. At one time they brought happiness. They are objects of such value—monetary, sentimental, or otherwise—that these folks put them in a safe deposit box to keep them secure, so that they would always know where these items are.

One day they bring these items to the bank, pay the bank for the safe-deposit box, carefully lay their treasures in the box, and then turn the key to keep them safe. And then on another day years later, they receive a letter from the bank saying that, because it has been a number of years since the rent on the box has been paid, the items must be claimed or they will be put up for auction. And that letter is simply put aside. Perhaps there are three tragedies in life: to lose one's heart's desire, to gain it, or simply, to walk away from it.

The longing that marks our lives is often mixed with nostalgia and can be mistaken for nostalgia. I tend to experience this longing at Christmas. As much as I revel in the season and drink it in, there is still what I can only call an unquenchable longing that stands near the center of the season. Sometimes that takes shape as longing for other Christmases, but it is more than mere nostalgia for some perfect Christmas of my past, because I cannot remember a Christmas that seemed complete. There was never a Christmas in my memory that did not bring with it a measure of this longing.

If asked to reconstruct a Christmas from my memories, here is what I would picture: My father and mother are there. My Aunt Tudy is there, as she was every year after her husband died. My grandmother is there, sitting quietly in the corner, taking so long to unwrap her gifts that the children can take naps before she is finished.

In addition to these four, who all died years ago, my brother and sister and their families, my wife, Karen, and I and our children are all somehow there in this Christmas of my memory. Aunt Tudy takes my daughter, Alanna, in her lap to tell her a story, even though she died before Alanna was born and Alanna is too old to crawl onto anyone's lap for a story anymore. My father shares a joke with his grandson, Todd, as surely as he would have if he had ever lived to see him. My grandmother's memory, which escaped her entirely during her last years, is restored at this Christmas, and she is once again able to tell the story about how my grandfather courted her for only ten days before proposing marriage. And, somehow, my grandfather himself is there as well, although he died several months before I was born. That is, in this Christmas of my memory, in this Christmas of my longing, all the broken and scattered pieces of life are gathered up and put together in ways that were never possible in any "real" Christmas.

This is something more than mere nostalgia, and more profound as well, because what we long for is not merely a Christmas from our past, but a gathering up of our past, present, and future into a harmony that is not achieved in the days of our lives. What we desire is not merely to be with those we love but to be united with them in a way that is not possible even when they are present. It is to be together in ways that are impossible in this life, and we can only barely approach in our dreams. What we long for is to have the broken and scattered pieces brought together in ways that we are unable to do. And that is why I have concluded that our longing—what can feel something like homesickness—is, in some way, a yearning for God.

It is a desire and a yearning for a special kind of homecoming, not just to be home with loved ones, but to find home with God, the one the psalmist calls "our dwelling place in all generations" (Psalm 90:1).

Elsewhere, the psalmist cries, "As a deer longs for flowing streams, so my soul longs for you, O God" (Psalm 42:1).

I am convinced that we all long for the presence of God with a deep, aching hunger, a hunger as sure as the hunger for food, but with this difference—we do not always know how to fill it. We do not always know what we are looking for.

Saint Augustine observed that our hearts are restless until they find the rest that is found only in God. Philosopher Blaise Pascal made a similar point by saying that each of us is born with

> ✦✦✦✦✦✦✦✦✦
>
> What we long for is to have the broken and scattered pieces brought together in ways that we are unable to do. And that is why I have concluded that our longing—what can feel something like homesickness—is, in some way, a yearning for God.

an empty place in our hearts—a void—that is in the shape of God, and that means that nothing and no one else can entirely or ultimately fill it. This empty space is not a square hole or anything as simple as that, but a complex, hungering, God-shaped space where only God fits and only God can fill. We can try to fill that space with other things—human relationships, careers, or other earthly pursuits—but they will sooner or later leave us unsatisfied. Which means that our task is to learn what we are looking for and whom we are looking for.

After all, if that empty space implanted in our soul is in the shape of God, then our attempts to fill it with anything else will leave empty corners that will ache.

So Jesus asks at critical junctures in his life and ministry, "What are you looking for?" and "Who are you looking for?"

And even in the afterglow of Easter it is still his question: "Who are you looking for?"

Obviously, Jesus thinks this is a question worth repeating, as if in some way it is *the* question.

CHAPTER 2

A QUESTION ABOUT COMPASSION

✦✦✦✦✦✦✦✦✦

A MINISTER I WORK WITH FREQUENTLY REMINDS me that everyone has a basic human need to be seen, that is, to be understood and valued. So she articulates that one of her primary
goals in working with the youth of our church is to make them
feel truly seen. If someone in the congregation is particularly grumpy, my colleague will say, "She just wants to be seen
in her unhappiness." If someone else has drifted away from
the church, she will offer this explanation: "I don't think he
felt seen here." My colleague goes on to conclude, "You can't
fake truly seeing another person. People know if you really
see them or not. When you truly see them, you find their note,
their vibration, their connection with God, and you dance with
them right there."

But it is not always easy to see another person. Sometimes we can observe someone and still not see him or her. To
see someone in the fullest sense requires a receptivity and

openness to the other—just who that person is, as he or she is—which often are beyond us.

Most of my early life was spent within the gravitational field of New York City and a good deal of time in the city itself. A while back I was going to see a play with some friends from other parts of the country, friends who are less familiar with the city's sometimes strange and difficult ways. As we walked to the theatre I had a certain spring in my step. After all, I was with people I enjoy, the exhilarating rhythms of the city were all around us, and I had in my pocket tickets to the hottest show in town.

To get to the theatre we had to walk through a somewhat tough neighborhood. No problem, I assured my companions. I've done it many times. Conversation flowed. There was much laughter. And then I realized that my companions had become suddenly silent. Something had obviously happened, but I did not know what. Then one friend said, "Did you see that woman? She looked like a prostitute. Did you see the way she was crying?" Everyone else immediately responded, obviously struck by the same sight.

We walked the next few blocks in silence. The reason for my silence was probably different, however. I had also seen the woman who so haunted the others, but in a sense I didn't see her at all. Somehow, in all the times I had walked in that neighborhood and ones like it, I had lost some of my ability to see. Do you see this woman? Of course, she's right in front of me. No, I mean do you actually see this woman? Well...no, not really.

On another occasion, this time in a suburb of New York,

I stood with another friend before the enormous front door of a big house, waiting for someone to let us in. In some ways it looked like a gracious manor house that had seen better days, a proud dowager who was now a bit down on her luck. From where it is perched there is a privileged view of the majestic Hudson River, the same river that has inspired so many artists and once drew the Roosevelts, Vanderbilts, and other famous families to build grand mansions on its banks.

Finally, someone dressed in a uniform opened the door and summoned us inside. There in the entranceway, we were asked to sign a book, something like an enormous guest book, heavy as a millstone, with yellowed pages that must have gone back years.

Then we had to show our IDs, were frisked, and were told to walk through a metal detector, much as one would do in an airport. But that is where the comparison ends. As I emerged through the metal detector, a woman behind a large desk barked: "Wait! I told you to wait. Pay attention! You are not listening to me. Do it again." All I could think to say is, "Yes, ma'am." I certainly did not want to do anything to provoke her further.

I was learning that in addition to being difficult to get out of Sing Sing, it is not easy to get in either. Sing Sing is a prison just north of New York City on the Hudson River. In fact, that's where the expression "up the river" comes from. If you are found guilty of a violent crime you are sent "up the river" to Sing Sing, a maximum security facility for those prisoners doing "hard time" for violent crimes. It is also called "The Big House" for reasons I can now understand.

I was there at the invitation of Bonnie Rosborough, who, in addition to her ministry at a church in suburban New York, teaches a class, offered by New York Theological Seminary, for prisoners at Sing Sing. It is the only master's degree program offered in a prison in this country. The members of the class are studying to be ministers, and this particular course is called "Foundations of Ministry." It meets for two and a half hours every Wednesday afternoon on the prison grounds.

The students in that class were reading a book I coauthored with another minister, Lillian Daniel, *This Odd and Wondrous Calling*. The book offers some personal reflections on the vocation of pastoral ministry. Pastor Bonnie, as she is called, invited us to visit the class, and we eagerly accepted the invitation. Both Lillian and I had taught seminarians before but, obviously, in very different settings from this.

I tried not to have too many preconceived notions about the members of the class, who had all been found guilty of a violent crime, but I was not entirely successful in my efforts. Try as I might to stay open, I did have a picture of these men in my mind, even though I had never been in such an environment before. I pictured that the men in the class would be hardened by their experience, guarded, maybe sullen or cynical, perhaps even scornful of these two suburban ministers coming to meet with them. After all, what would we have to say that would be of interest or relevance to their lives?

Pastor Bonnie looks something like the actress Bea Arthur in her prime and carries herself with some of the same authoritative nonchalance. As we waited for all of the security measures to be completed, I asked her, "What do the men in the class make of our coming today?" She replied, "Oh, they're really looking forward to it. They have so little interaction with the outside world. They often feel forgotten, invisible, locked up with the key thrown away."

Finally, we were cleared for entrance. We were escorted

❖❖❖❖❖❖❖❖❖

I had smuggled something into the prison. I clung to it. I was determined to keep it close throughout my time there. I smuggled into Sing Sing a particular question Jesus asks.

through many doors that all shut behind us with a decisive clang. I did not let on to the security guards that, unbeknownst to them, I had smuggled something into the prison. I clung to it. I was determined to keep it close throughout my time there. I smuggled into Sing Sing a particular question Jesus asks. He asks it at a dinner party at the home of a Pharisee named Simon (Luke 7:36-50).

While they are eating dinner, a woman, who is described only as a sinner, crashes the party, falls at Jesus' feet, and begins to bathe his feet with her tears. She also lets down her hair, a most intimate gesture that would be taboo for women of the time, and she uses her hair to dry Jesus' feet. Her actions only add to the scandal of her being there in the first place.

Because this woman is known as a sinner, Pharisees and other people of polite company have nothing to do with her. Upright people act as if she does not exist. These conventions are so strong that Simon simply assumes that Jesus must not recognize that she is a sinner. Simon concludes that Jesus does not see the woman for who she is, because if he did he would treat her as if she were invisible.

Jesus asks, "Do you see this woman?" In this setting and in this company, it is a probing and challenging question. The woman may be right in front of them, but that does not mean they all see her. Sometimes people choose not to see. There is, after all, a cost to seeing. If you see this woman, actually see this woman, you might need to move beyond the stereotypes and preconceptions. You might have to stop simply labeling her a sinner and then leaving it at that. You might have to relate to her as a person, as one soul to another soul. You might have to respond to her with compassion.

Simon only sees what sort of woman she is. Jesus does not see a sort of woman; he sees this woman. The question Jesus asks—"Do you see this woman?"—challenges those around him to see her as well.

At Sing Sing, the room where the class is taught looked like a basement room in an old church where there is a lot of deferred maintenance—cinder-block walls, peeling paint, a leaky steam radiator that hissed like a snake. But I only saw that later. What I saw at first were the prisoners who got up to shake our hands, to thank us for coming, to ask, "Would you like a glass of water or some tea?" I just wasn't expecting that.

We sat down. Pastor Bonnie introduced us to the class and then asked the prisoners to introduce themselves. The man in the group who has served the least time had been in Sing Sing for fifteen years, others much longer. At least one man had been in that prison for over thirty years. (I try to remember what I was doing thirty years ago.) Some are serving life sentences.

The members of the class had prepared for our visit, and the prisoners' first question was about the basis of pastoral authority. I have learned from my work with seminarians and new pastors that this is often the question that infuses much of those early years of ministry. I still found it curious that this was the first question in this setting. But then the teacher asked the members of the class, "What are the signs of authority here?"

"Handcuffs, badges, nightsticks," one man said. "Guns. Mace," said another. So, yes, what is the source of a pastor's authority when you don't have any of those things?

Whatever preconceived notions I had brought with me disappeared almost instantly. We were warmly welcomed by the men in the class. They were eager to engage with the book and with us. Several of the men were so articulate, if you closed your eyes, you might think you were in a seminary classroom at Yale or Princeton. When Pastor Bonnie asked the class, "What is your definition of evil?" one student (I mean, prisoner) gave a definition that was so thoughtful and brilliantly phrased that Pastor Bonnie came back, "George, did you get that answer from a catechism or something?" He said, "No, I got it from my head."

At one point, one of the men said, "So, Martin, in the book you wrote about your wife. How is she? And did she ever go back to that room where she made the banners for worship?"— which is a story I told in the book. He wanted to know how the story ended. Another man asked my coauthor, "Lillian, how is your son with diabetes?"

We also learned that the prisoners had raised over six

thousand dollars for a local food pantry from the twenty-two cents an hour they received for doing menial work. They had also earned enough money to provide back-to-school kits— which included items such as pencils and even backpacks— to children who visited the prison. One of the members of the class challenged us, "What are you or your church doing to guide the youth? I think there is a crisis among the youth today." He was respectful but firm in following up on my rather lame answer to his question. Here, on the inside, he was challenging us to tend to those on the outside. He was concerned about justice, and not merely criminal justice.

Referring to a sinner before him, Jesus asked, "Do you see this woman?" That is the question that was whispered in my ear as we met with the men in the class: "Do you see this man?" Can you clear away the stereotypes and the preconceived notions and the condemnations long enough to see this man? After all, the thick and towering walls of the prison are not the only thing preventing you from seeing these men.

As the time approached for the class to end, one of the students spoke up and said, "I'm sorry, Pastor Bonnie, but we have only fifteen minutes to go. I want to make sure we get our books signed before it's too late. Then, if we've got some time, we can come back to this discussion." And at that they all stood up and formed a line. They all wanted their books signed.

So I signed each book, with each man's name and these words, "With every good wish and best blessing, Martin." And, unlike other times when I have signed books, after I finished writing in each book, I did not remain seated. I stood up from the table to shake each man's hand. I wanted to be able to look each one in the eyes. I wanted, for once, as best as I could, to be able to answer Jesus' question: "Do you see this man?"

As we were heading out the door, George made a beeline for me and said, "Pastor Copenhaver, at some point I would like to talk with you about Yale Divinity School." (He had read in our book a reference to Yale, which is where I went to seminary.) I said, "Sure, George, give me a call when you get out," although I thought it unlikely that I would ever hear from him.

Then, about eighteen months later, I got a phone call: "Pastor Copenhaver, this is George. I've just been released from Sing Sing. I'm back home in Albany working with a street ministry here, but I wondered if we can talk some about Yale Divinity School." I suggested that the next time I was heading to Yale, I would give him a call so he might meet me there for a tour and perhaps an interview.

A couple of months later, I called him back: "George, I'm going to Yale a week from Friday. Might that work for you?"

"Oh, that would be wonderful, Pastor. The only thing is, I have to get approval from my parole officer to cross state lines, and he needs a little more time than that." It had never occurred to me. Clearly, I was new at this.

The next time I planned to go to Yale, I gave George more notice: "Could you meet me there four weeks from now?"

"Absolutely, Pastor. I will be there."

When the day arrived, we met in the stately rotunda outside the chapel of the divinity school. He wore a blue silk tie and a neatly ironed shirt. In other words, he looked like what he was—a student dressed for an interview. He wore a name tag that was given to him by campus security when he arrived.

George and I sat together at the chapel service, and then he went off to visit a class and to have a tour and an interview. At the end of the day we met on the lush and manicured lawn in the quadrangle of the school. It had been a good day, he said. He was definitely going to apply. I wished him well, and we parted.

During the following weeks I would occasionally get text messages or phone calls from George, bringing me up-to-date on his progress.

Then I got a call from the dean of the Divinity School: "Martin, we have an application that is a little unusual for us, and we are trying to figure out what to do. Since you are a reference, I thought I would call you. It's about George. On the one hand, he is a convicted felon, and we have the rest of the YDS community to consider. On the other hand, we are a divinity school, and obviously, we believe in redemption. So I am wondering what you can tell me about him."

So I told the dean how I knew George and what I knew about him. He replied, "Well, that's all I need."

The next day I got a call from George: "Pastor, I just got a call from Yale Divinity School. They admitted me."

A month later I got another call: "Pastor, I just got a call from Yale Divinity School. They've given me a full scholarship."

Several months later, I was preaching at the national gathering of my denomination, the United Church of Christ. I preached on the passage in which Jesus is at dinner with polite company, looks at a sinner, and asks, "Do you see this woman?" I talked about the importance of seeing those around us. And I told about my visit to Sing Sing and my eagerness to see—really see—the men I encountered there, particularly because I am not always good at that kind of seeing.

I don't know how George found that sermon on the Internet, but he did. The day after I gave that sermon, he sent me a text message: "Hi Pastor Copenhaver. Just listened to your sermon from the UCC Synod this past weekend. It moved me in a very emotional way. Thank you for seeing me. May I now see people, too. I went to Sing Sing a few weeks ago for the New York Theological School graduation and saw Dr. Rosborough. I hope the men felt I saw them, too. Already signed my lease. I'll be in New Haven mid-August, and I start at Yale later that month. Thank you for sharing our story. May we all see as Jesus does. What a difference we can make. Just look at my life."

"Do you see this woman?" That question unsettles not just when visiting unfamiliar places, like a maximum security prison. After all, it is expected that socially aware Christians would feel some guilt about how we ignore the poor and oppressed and how we fail to see the marginalized.

The question becomes even more unsettling when it is brought home: "Do you see this woman?" The question comes uncomfortably close when I ask it about my wife or my daughter or my son. Do I see them as they really are? Do I see them as Jesus sees them? There is a reason why I have glasses that help me see what is distant and also what is very close, because both the distant and the close can be difficult for me to see without some help.

The question comes even closer when I ask it of myself: do I really see this man? Of course, the answer is both yes and no. I know myself well enough to know that there is much about myself I choose not to see. To see myself clearly, without illusion, would be too overwhelming.

So it is a lacerating question, and also a reassuring one, for behind it is an answer, and the answer is that Jesus sees. Jesus sees my formerly incarcerated friend as he really is. Jesus sees the members of my family as they really are. I might look at my wife and see all that might make me doubt her love for me, but Jesus sees her in all the ways she loves me. I might sometimes look at my daughter and see only her accomplishments and not her fears, but Jesus sees her fully. I might look at my son and still see the boy he was in ways that obscure my view of the man he has become. And Jesus sees me as I really am. Knowing that can be disquieting. But when I am able to be quiet and see Jesus for who he is, it is a knowledge that comforts, deeply. Jesus is the one who sees fully and yet loves completely. That assurance is the rare gift in his question.

CHAPTER 3

A QUESTION ABOUT IDENTITY

❖❖❖❖❖❖❖❖❖

"**WHAT IS YOUR NAME?**" **IS THAT A SIMPLE** question, or is it a profound one? Well, it depends on the circumstances and who is asking the question. If you tell a maitre d' at a restaurant that you have a reservation and he asks, "What is your name?" the question could hardly be more straightforward. But when Jesus asks the question, "What is your name?"—as he asks the possessed man in Mark 5 and Luke 8—it is quite a different matter. After all, to know another's name is the beginning of relationship.

Names are more than mere labels. We identify with our names. In a sense, we are our names. Shakespeare's Juliet famously asked, "What's in a name?" Then she answered her own question: "That which we call a rose by any other word would smell as sweet." But if Juliet can easily contemplate changing the name of a rose it is probably because she is not a rose herself. She would not be nearly so casual if the name to be changed were her own. If someone insisted on calling her Julie or Jules she might well protest.

I think of all the ways my own name has been changed, however inadvertently. My father used to collect misspellings and mispronunciations of our family's name. His collection was particularly extensive because for many years he had a radio program, so he would receive letters from people who had heard his name only once. Variations such as Copenhaven and Copenhagen seemed predictable enough, but Copenheimer also was popular. People seemed especially creative with the latter syllables of our name, I suppose figuring that if they made it into the third syllable they were home free. That is the only way I can explain Copenschlitz, which I think was only used once but has lived on in our family's oral history.

We continue to expand my father's collection. In recent years our family name seems to have gone international, becoming Slavic (Copenhavek) and even Hispanic (Copenhavez). Although the members of my family have had a few laughs over these, I do not know anyone who takes their own name casually. As novelist Frederick Buechner observed, "If somebody mispronounces my name in some foolish way, I have the feeling that what's foolish is me."[7]

Many people I know have a version of their first name they do not like. A friend named Michael recoils from Mike. Another friend named Lillian visibly winces at the sound of Lilly. Then again, I know another Lillian who insists on being called Lilly.

Many people have called me Marty...once. I always correct

◆◆◆◆◆◆◆◆◆

We are intimately tied to our names in ways that are powerful and even rather mysterious.

-26-

them: "My friends call me Martin." I don't like being rude, but I dislike the name Marty even more. Perhaps my parents inculcated in me a dislike of the name Marty because I was born the same year the movie *Marty* won the Academy Award for best picture. In that film Ernest Borgnine plays the title role, a homely butcher from Brooklyn; so perhaps my parents were intent on disassociating their new baby from that movie character who was so well known at the time. But there is more to it. Quite simply, Marty is not my name. I do not feel addressed by it. It is someone else's name.

We are intimately tied to our names in ways that are powerful and even rather mysterious. Buechner testifies to this mystery: "If my name were different, I would be different."[8] Parents who are expecting a child often experience this. In deciding upon a name for their unborn child, they may consider the names within their families or search for a name by perusing a book of baby's names. Through that exercise, however, parents can get the sense that they are not so much choosing a name, but rather seeking to discover the name the child has already, a name that is not yet known to them. When our first child, Alanna, was born, there seemed no way that she could have any other name. She was and is Alanna, and to this day people will say to her, "You just look so much like an Alanna." I am not sure I know what that means, exactly, but I know it is true. Alanna embodies her name. She *is* Alanna.

By contrast, I also know parents who settled comfortably on a name only to change it soon after their child was born because the name did not seem to fit. My wife's given name is Karen, but she says that it has never really felt like her name.

She does not feel addressed by it. The name she feels most addressed by—the name that feels as though it fits her—is the nickname I gave her in college. I was rehearsing for a two-man play when we were first dating, and she helped me learn my lines. I would recite my lines, and she would read the lines of the other character, whose name was Charlie, and it just stuck. I have called her Charlie ever since, and even though no else calls her Charlie, she says it is the name she feels most addressed by.

My father always called my mother Susie, even though her name was Marian, and did so from a very early stage in their relationship. He said she just always looked like a Susie to him. My father was the only one to use the nickname, so after he died, there was no one left to call my mother Susie. After he was gone, she was called Marian, except in her dreams. In her dreams, she told us, she was still called Susie.

Not all nicknames stick, of course, and that may be particularly true of nicknames you try to give yourself. When I was in grade school, my best friend was David Smith, who wanted to be called Smitty. At that time I longed to be called Copie, which had been my father's nickname in college. So we made a pact: I would always call him Smitty and he would always call me Copie, and if either of us used any other name for the other we would get a punch on the arm. Obviously, whoever came up with the children's rhyme, "Sticks and stones may break my bones, but names will never hurt me," had never entered into a pact like that. After a time, with arms bruised, we simply agreed to go back to calling each other David and Martin.

My fifth-grade church school teacher, Mr. Popma, was a distinguished gentleman who wore a pin-striped suit with a crisp handkerchief in his pocket every Sunday. At the beginning of the first class, he peered over his reading glasses and asked us what we each wanted to be called. No one had ever asked me that before. Mr. Popma was not asking the usual question, "What do people call you?" Instead, he was asking what each of us wanted to be called. No one had ever asked me that before. I saw my chance. "Copie," I said. From that day on he always called me Copie, but he is the only one who ever did, leaving me feeling a bit like the character in Dylan Thomas's *Under Milk Wood* who was "kissed once by the pigsty when she wasn't looking and was never kissed again although she was looking all the time." Eventually, I simply gave up wanting to be called Copie. Apparently, it is just not my name.

Names distinguish us from others. My grandfather, father, and brother were all named Charles Leonard Copenhaver, but my grandfather was known as Leonard, my father was Charles, and my brother is called Chad. They could share a name, but, as with many families, they each were given their own variation of that shared name. OK, the boxer George Foreman did name all five of his sons George, but that is largely considered a quirky curiosity. For the most part, we do not want to share our names. If I meet someone else named Martin, the name tends to stick on my tongue, as if there is something not quite right about it, as if this person stole the name or assumed it under false pretenses. We want our names to distinguish us.

We put up with name tags, even tacky ones that say (and seem to scream), "Hello! My name is . . ." because we recognize that it is hard for any kind of relationship, even a casual one, to develop if you do not know each other's names. If someone does not bother to learn your name, it is an indication that he doesn't really care a fig about other aspects of your life, either.

This is also why it is painful to have your name forgotten. Buechner, who has obviously given a lot of thought to this naming business, writes, "If somebody forgets my name, I feel it's I who am forgotten."[9] Indeed, if someone does not remember your name, it can make you feel small and insignificant. For the most part, we remember the names of important people or people who are important to us. So it can be particularly painful to have a loved one forget your name, even if there is a medical reason for the loss of memory.

It is almost axiomatic that nothing is as musical to the ear as the sound of one's own name. If that is true, it is not from sheer vanity. Rather, we long to be addressed, for words to find us where we live. Each of us wants to be recognized as an individual. We yearn to be known and known by name. The use of one's name symbolizes such ties between people and can actually help create them.

So when Scripture says that God calls each one by name, it comes as a welcome assurance. It implies that God is not an impersonal force. If God knows me by name, it means that God is a being and, what is more, a being who seeks to be in relationship with me. It is one of God's ways of reaching out to me—not just me, of course, but me in all of my particularity, who I really am. That's why, when God calls me by name, I am quite sure God uses the name I feel most addressed by, the name I hear in my dreams. That is, when God calls me by name, I don't think God says Rev. Copenhaver or Marty. Rather, God calls me Martin because that's not just my name. It is who I am.

One of Jesus' parables, commonly called "Lazarus and the Rich Man" (Luke 16:19-31), includes an interesting—and telling—use of names. Lazarus is a beggar who sits at the gate of the rich man's house watching his guests arrive in their fancy clothes for the sumptuous feast that the parable says the rich man enjoyed every night. Lazarus does not long to be invited to the feast, or anything as grand as that, but just wants to get a few scraps of bread that have been tossed on the floor.

Jesus begins the parable, "There was a certain rich man..." The rich man's name is not given, which should tip us off from the beginning that something different is going on here, because rich people's names generally are known and known quite well. If you are rich, it seems that everyone knows your name. The names of rich people often are spoken like magic words. Those names have the power to open closed doors. And yet, Jesus gives no name to the rich man in the parable.

It is safe to assume that the rich man of the parable does not know the name of the beggar who sits at the gate of his house. But in the parable (as in the eyes of God, of course), the beggar has a name—Lazarus, a name that means "God helps." It is a rather poignant name, for clearly no one but God made an effort to help him. It is the only time Jesus ever uses a name in a parable. To the rich man, the beggar is nameless, just a person to be ignored, invisible. But to God he has a name. He is not known as "a beggar." He is Lazarus.

Like so much of Jesus' teachings, this parable upends the usual order of things. In the world, rich men's names are known and beggars are often treated as nameless. In the parable, as in God's realm, it is the beggar, of all people, who is addressed by name.

Then we come to the dramatic encounter between Jesus and a man with an "unclean spirit" (Mark 5:1-20). Mark says that the man is possessed by demons, but many of the behaviors he describes also could be symptoms of serious mental illness, specifically multiple personality disorder. In either case, the poor fellow clearly is suffering. He lives in a graveyard. He has been ostracized by everyone alive and now lives among the dead. He was put in chains, to protect others from his violent outbursts, and perhaps to protect himself, as well. He is so agitated and strong, however, that he was able to wrench the chains apart. Now he howls like a beast and pounds his own body with stones.

When the man sees Jesus from a distance, however, he runs to him and bows down before him. Jesus asks, "What is your name?" This is not a trifling question, and particularly in this instance. It is the question one human being asks another. It is the beginning of relationship. This man has been exiled from his community and has been left for dead. We can only imagine how long it has been since he has been asked his name. Probably he has not been asked for all the time he has been tormented, and that in itself has added to the torment. During his time of distress he has been known by labels rather than by a name: a madman, a demoniac, a dangerous beast. But Jesus asks, "What is your name?" Under these circumstances, the question sounds like nothing less than an invitation to life, the first step in healing.

The man replies, "Legion is my name." It is another poignant name. A legion was a unit of the Roman army of six thousand soldiers. They often brutalized those who lived in occupied lands. So when the man says, "Legion is my name," he is testifying to how many demons occupy his soul and how destructive they can all be.

Then, in an odd twist to the story, Jesus commands the demons to leave the man alone and to enter a huge herd of pigs instead. The pigs then madly trot off the edge of a cliff into the sea.

✦✦✦✦✦✦✦✦✦

Like so much of Jesus' teachings, this parable upends the usual order of things. In the world, rich men's names are known and beggars are often treated as nameless. In the parable, as in God's realm, it is the beggar, of all people, who is addressed by name.

The man, now in a new set of clothes and in his right mind, asks if he can follow Jesus on his travels. Jesus has another idea. He tells the man to go to his home so that his friends and family can hear this amazing story and see the transformation for themselves.

So the man goes back into his hometown and does just that. He tells the story of the miraculous thing that has happened and about how he has been restored to life. I imagine him beginning his story by saying, with something like wonder, "The first thing Jesus did was to ask me, 'What is your name?'"

CHAPTER 4

QUESTIONS ABOUT FAITH AND DOUBT

❖❖❖❖❖❖❖❖❖

JESUS IS WITH HIS DISCIPLES IN A BOAT HEADING across the Sea of Galilee. It is a bit of a break from the clamorous crowds and the press of human need. Jesus falls asleep. In Mark's version of this story, he includes the charming detail that Jesus falls asleep in the stern of the boat with his head on a pillow (Mark 4:35-41). I suppose Jesus is sleeping what is sometimes called "the sleep of the innocent" or "the sleep of the righteous"—that is, sleep with a clear conscience, so a deep and blissful sleep—because even when a severe storm tosses the boat as if it were a mere toy, Jesus is able to remain asleep. Even the shouting wind does not awaken him.

The drama of the scene is captured in Rembrandt van Rijn's famous painting "The Storm on the Sea of Galilee." In Rembrandt's rendering, the boat seems like the very definition of tempest-tossed. Enormous waves are leaping into the boat. It is clear to everyone—both the seasoned fishermen and the landlubbers on their maiden voyage—that they are in great peril. One disciple holds onto the mast for dear life. Another in a red shirt and with a decidedly green face holds onto the gunwale and heaves over the side of the boat.

There is a stark contrast in the painting between the bow of the boat and the stern. The left side of the painting, the bow of the boat, is light and charged with drama. The enormous waves are white and peaked, almost as if they are watery mountaintops. The bodies of the men on this side of the boat are contorted as they try to lower a sail or merely to hang on. If you focus on this side of the painting long enough you can almost hear the wind howl and feel a bit queasy yourself.

By contrast, on the right side of the painting, in the stern of the boat, there is a circle of calm around Jesus. In most of his works Rembrandt depicts Jesus in the light and often as a source of light, but here all the light is in the bow of the ship where the storm rages, while Jesus is in the darker part of the scene. It is Rembrandt's way of depicting Jesus as the center of calm, as if Jesus is the very eye of the storm.

In the foreground, on the border between the contrasting sides of the painting, is another figure, who has slapped his hand up to his forehead, as if imitating Homer Simpson's famous gesture and accompanying exclamation, "D'oh!" If this were a photograph, he would be looking straight at the camera, his expression saying, "How did I get into this mess?" (with probably a few expletives thrown in). If you look closely, you can clearly see that this figure is Rembrandt. He put himself in the scene. That is why there are fourteen figures in the boat: Jesus, twelve disciples, and Rembrandt.

It is telling where Rembrandt puts himself—right on the border between the threatening storm in the bow of the boat and the circle of calm around Jesus in the stern of the boat. Rembrandt is right on the border, perhaps because he identifies with both the fear and the faith.

The painting depicts the very moment the disciples are waking up Jesus. The hand of one disciple is on Jesus' shoulder, obviously to rouse him. In Luke's version of the story, the disciples say, "Master, master, we are perishing!" (Luke 8:22-25). In Mark's version the plea is even more poignant: "Teacher, do you not care that we are perishing?"

Jesus is anything but sympathetic. First, he takes care of business. He rebukes the wind and the raging waves, and they calm down. In Luke's version, he then turns to his disciples: "Where is your faith?" Mark records Jesus asking, "Why are you afraid? Have you still no faith?"

These are exasperated questions. Jesus sounds almost indignant, which seems rather harsh under the circumstances. I picture one or more of the disciples wanting to respond, "Where is your faith? Let me see, I must have put it here somewhere...Where is your faith!?! Seriously? My faith was being tossed around by a violent storm that was about to take us down!"

Jesus' responses are similar when Peter attempts to walk on water (Matthew 14:22-33). The disciples are once again in a boat on the Sea of Galilee. Jesus has sent them ahead without him, but none of the disciples thought to ask how he would join them so far out on the water. They are terrified when they see his figure through the mist, walking on water. Unlike a sailor who asks permission to come on board, Peter asks Jesus' permission to get out of the boat: "Lord, if it's you, order me to come to you on the water." Jesus says, "Come." At that Peter vaults out of the boat and begins to walk on the water to Jesus.

Peter is doing quite well for a time. When the wind kicks up, however, he panics and begins to sink. I picture Peter like a young boy on his first bike ride without training wheels. He rides along just fine until he thinks, "I can't be doing this!" After that moment of panic he cannot help but wobble to a slow and awkward fall by the side of the road.

When Peter begins to sink and pleads for help, Jesus stretches out his hand, fishes him out of the water, and asks, "You of little faith, why did you doubt?" It is another exasperated question.

Peter must have been tempted to respond with some questions of his own: "Why did I doubt? Don't you think that's a silly question? Why did I doubt? Because I was walking on water, that's why."

So why is Jesus so impatient with his disciples' lack of faith?

Jesus is exasperated because his disciples' lack of faith is a denigration of his relationship with them. If I say of another person, "I have faith in her," I mean many things, including, "I trust her; I rely on her; I love her; I depend on her." To have faith in Jesus, then, implies a whole range of ways one actively relates to him. It is the language of relationship. Faith is a living, dynamic relationship that is more akin to trust than anything else.

Jesus is impatient with his followers' lack of faith because it really comes down to a lack of trust. It's not like other short-comings exhibited by the disciples. It's personal.

Jesus obviously feels he has earned the trust of his disciples. If you have exhibited trustworthiness over time, it can hurt to realize that you are still not fully trusted. I think that is what is going on with Jesus here. He is not just frustrated with his disciples' lack of faith. He is hurt by it. He is responding as if it is personal, and, in a sense, it is.

It is as if Jesus is saying, "After all we have been through together, after all I have taught you, after all you have observed in me, after all the deep and abiding love I have shown you and promised you . . . after all of that, you do not trust me? Where is your faith?"

We often use the words *belief* and *faith* as if they are synonymous, but they are different, and the differences matter.

William Sloane Coffin put it this way: "Faith isn't believing without proof—it's trusting without reservation."

Imagine you are at a circus. A skilled high-wire artist has accomplished so many marvelous feats that the audience has come to believe that he can do almost anything. The ringmaster addresses the crowd: "Ladies and gentlemen, how many of you believe that this daring man can ride safely over the high wire on his bicycle while carrying someone on his shoulders? If you believe he can do it, please raise your hand!" If you were in the audience you might raise your hand along with all the others, a great silent chorus of belief. "Very well, then," says the ringmaster, seeing an almost unanimous vote of confidence, "now who will be the first to volunteer to sit on his shoulders?"

The difference between belief and faith is the difference

between staying in your seat and volunteering to climb on the shoulders of the high-wire artist. Ultimately, faith is not about believing certain things; it is about putting our trust in someone.

Some of our confusion about the nature of faith can be attributed to a quirk in the English language. The English language is the only European language that does not have a verb form of the word *faith*. In English we cannot say, "I faith, you faith, and he or she faiths."

This one small characteristic of the English language can cause a lot of confusion. Since, in English, there is no verb form for the word *faith*, we must choose between two options, and either option can mislead us about the nature of faith. The first option is that we can settle for "I believe." But that blurs the distinction between faith and belief, a distinction that should be retained. The second option is to use *faith* as a noun. We can say, for instance, "I have faith." But if we do that, we have implied that faith is a possession. Consider the implications: if I say I "have" something—a pen, a nose, or whatever—that implies a certain permanence or certainty. You either have it, or you do not have it. Faith, however, is not a possession; it is a capacity, a capacity for trust that is not nearly so permanent. Our faith is stronger on some days than it is on other days.

◆◆◆◆◆◆◆◆◆

Faith, properly understood, is a verb. Faith is something we do. Indeed, if language would allow, we would say something like this: "I faith sometimes. I wish I could faith more often. In fact, I'm working toward faithing in God in all that I do."

We can live out our faith more completely at some times than at other times.

Faith, properly understood, is a verb. Faith is something we do. Indeed, if language would allow, we would say something like this: "I faith sometimes. I wish I could faith more often. In fact, I'm working toward faithing in God in all that I do." That may be grammatically painful, but it is theologically correct. Faith is not something we have with certainty, once and for all, at all times, under all circumstances. Rather, it is something we do, sometimes more easily than others, sometimes more completely than other times. Human frailty rarely allows us more than that. We are all capable of acting faithfully, but none of us is faithful always. If faith is a noun, a thing to possess, then some of us have it, and others of us do not. But if we properly understand *faith* as a verb, it is something we do—on occasion, at least.

As Peter attempts to walk on water toward Jesus, he faiths pretty well for a while, but then fear tracks him down and takes over. As Peter faiths less and less, he sinks more and more. Even then, however, despite his fears and doubts, Peter can still faith a little. That is, he is capable of some trust, even if not complete trust. He is able to faith long enough and well enough to cry out, "Lord, save me!" His faith does not save him, because his faith is not constant. But he is saved, despite his fickle faith.

Jesus does not expect his followers to trust that he will calm every storm. And, sure enough, after that day on the Sea of Galilee, his disciples do continue to face every manner of storm—literal storms, of course, but also storms of rejection and violence, storms of inner turmoil. Jesus does not promise to protect his followers from all of that. He does, however, want his followers to exhibit the kind of trust that allowed the Apostle Paul to affirm, "I am convinced that neither death, not life, nor angels, nor rulers, nor things present, nor things to come, nor powers, nor height, nor depth, nor anything else in all creation, will be able to separate us from the love of God in Christ Jesus our Lord" (Romans 8:38-39).

I was once asked to summarize the Christian gospel in seven words or less. My response was this: "God gets the last word." (I figured I would save the two additional words for another occasion when I really needed them.)

When I was asked to expand my summary of the gospel to seventy-five words, I replied: "In the death and resurrection of Jesus it is clear that our God is the kind of God who insists on having the last word. To be sure, the second-to-last word, which can be very powerful, can be given to something else—despair, estrangement, hurt, evil, even death. But our God insists on having the very last word, and that is always a word of hope, of reconciliation, of healing, of goodness, and of life."

On occasion I have had to hold onto that affirmation in the way I would clutch a life preserver while bobbing about in a stormy sea. One such occasion was a particular hospital visit I made early in my ministry. When I visited Dorothy, a beloved member of our church, her doctor had just left the room, leaving a dark cloud behind him. Even a young minister could not miss it. Dorothy was an actress with a big personality who was used to commanding a room, but not this room, not now. She said in a voice softer than I had ever heard her use, "Have a seat, Martin. We've just gotten some difficult news." I perched on one side of her hospital bed, and her husband, Ed, sat on the other side. Then the two of them relayed some of what they had just learned, news that they themselves could not yet begin to take in fully. Dorothy's cancer had recurred after years of remission. A most unwelcome visitor was back. Treatment would begin the following week.

For a moment the three of us sat in silence, while contraptions connected to Dorothy with wires and tubes continued a steady rhythm of drip and pulse and beep.

Then Dorothy, looking straight at Ed, said, "I'll be OK."

Ed replied with his deeply soothing voice, "I know you will be. The doctors assure me that you will..."

"No, Ed," she said, her voice gaining in strength, "I mean, I will be OK either way."

She did not elaborate, but of course, what she meant was that she would be OK if she lived and OK if she died.

Gratefully, Dorothy ended up living quite a number of years longer, but that was hardly certain on that day—or on any of the days that followed. You never know what a day may hold, which means you need to know something else, which Dorothy did.

I have thought back on that brief exchange so many times. From that time on, I began to see that there are two ways to provide reassurance in the presence of fear. One form of reassurance is to say that everything will be all right—the surgery will be successful, the relationship will be mended, the storm will pass, your worst fears will not be realized. But there are few circumstances when that kind of reassurance is ours to give. The other form of reassurance is to say that, if we hold fast to the love of God, come what may, God will remain and not let us go. God gets the last word. Or, as Dorothy put it, "I will be OK either way."

It is that kind of faith, I think, that Jesus was looking for from his friends, even in the midst of a most terrible storm.

CHAPTER 5

QUESTIONS ABOUT WORRY

✦✦✦✦✦✦✦✦✦

JESUS DOES NOT WANT YOU TO WORRY. In fact, he repeatedly insists that you not worry—not that his insistence helps very much. No one can stop worrying on command. But he does offer help in the presence of worry through—you guessed it—a series of questions.

It is telling that Jesus' longest discourse on a human emotion is about worry. That is particularly remarkable in light of all the other possibilities. He could have talked most extensively about sadness, fear, grief, loneliness, or shame. Instead, it is worry he addresses at length. He could have talked at greater length about positive emotions—emotions such as happiness, love, or gratitude. Of course, he addresses all of those emotions and more, but Jesus' longest discourse about any human emotion is reserved for worry.

The poet W. H. Auden famously dubbed the latter part of the twentieth century "the Age of Anxiety." It is clear from Jesus' attention to the subject, however, that worry has been an unwelcome guest in human hearts and minds from the very beginning:

Therefore I tell you, do not worry about your
life, what you will eat or what you will drink,
or about your body, what you will wear. Is not
life more than food, and the body more than
clothing? Look at the birds of the air; they
neither sow nor reap nor gather into barns, and
yet your heavenly Father feeds them. Are you
not of more value than they? And can any of
you by worrying add a single hour to your span
of life? And why do you worry about clothing?
Consider the lilies of the field, how they grow;
they neither toil nor spin, yet I tell you, even
Solomon in all his glory was not clothed like
one of these. But if God so clothes the grass
of the field, which is alive today and tomorrow is thrown into the oven, will he not much
more clothe you—you of little faith? Therefore do not worry, saying, "What will we eat?"
or "What will we drink?" or "What will we
wear?" For it is the Gentiles who strive for all
these things; and indeed your heavenly Father
knows that you need all these things. But strive
first for the kingdom of God and his righteous-
ness, and all these things will be given to you
as well. So do not worry about tomorrow, for
tomorrow will bring worries of its own. Today's
trouble is enough for today. (Matthew 6:25-34)

Like many preachers who followed him, Jesus uses a refrain throughout. No fewer than three times in this passage

Jesus says, "Do not worry." A refrain is used to drive home the central point of a sermon, but in this case the repetition may have another purpose as well: the refrain, "Do not worry," bears repeating because worry is not easily banished. Worry insinuates itself. It creeps up and settles in wherever it can. Worry is so persistent that the injunction, "Do not worry," needs to persist as well.

Physician and author Lewis Thomas observed, "We are, perhaps, uniquely among the earth's creatures, the worrying animal." I don't know if other animals worry—a bloodhound, for instance, looks pretty worried to me—but there can be no doubt that the human animal is a worrier.

Sometimes worries can even seem to breed. I asked a woman who was facing some challenges at home, "Are you worried about the situation?" She replied, "No, but I worry that it is already past the time when I should have started worrying."

Worry is such a waste of energy and, in most instances, so misplaced—at least, other people's worries are. Someone in my extended family, who is one of five children, says that when her mother writes a letter it is almost always exactly five paragraphs long. Each of the children gets a paragraph devoted to her worries about him or her. Five children, five paragraphs, many worries. She says the goal is not to end up in the lead paragraph because that means that you have gone to the top of their mother's worry list.

I used to think that was so silly. I could not relate to her worrying so about her children. But, of course, that was before I had children of my own.

If you dig down to the root meaning of the word *worry*,

the literal meaning is "to strangle." When life gets you by the throat, the chances are it is worry that is doing the strangling.

So we long for someone to free us from our worries. Clearly, that is why Jesus keeps repeating, "Do not worry." But here is the catch: if you are really worried about something, does it ever help when someone says, "Don't worry about it"? If you are consumed with worry and someone tells you not to worry, what is your response? It is not likely to be a sincere, "Thank you so much. That's a big help." A more fitting response might be sarcasm: "Don't worry? Oh, thanks. I didn't know I had a choice."

The counsel, "Don't worry," not only fails to address our worry but also can come across as dismissive. And we know that our own worries are not so easily dismissed. Other people's worries may seem silly, but our own worries are deadly serious. Deadly. Serious.

In fact, if someone tells me not to be worried, I can become suspicious: "Ladies and gentlemen, you will have noticed that we are experiencing an unusual amount of turbulence in our flight today, but let us assure you that there is no reason for concern." Hmm. I wasn't particularly worried before. But I wonder why the pilot felt the need to tell us that?

The power of Jesus' teaching

◆◆◆◆◆◆◆◆◆

Rhetorical questions are not like other questions. In fact, for a time printers used a different form of punctuation for rhetorical questions. It was an ordinary question mark turned around. That practice died out in the seventeenth century, but the point remains: rhetorical questions are different from other questions.

about worry does not come from the repeated injunction, "Do not worry." Rather, the power comes from the five rhetorical questions he asks in quick succession:

"Is not life more than food, and the body more than clothing?"

"Are you not of more value than [the birds of the air]?"

"Can any of you by worrying add a single hour to your span of life?"

"And why do you worry about clothing?"

"If God so clothes the grass of the field, which is alive today and tomorrow is thrown into the oven, will he not much more clothe you—you of little faith?"

Rhetorical questions are not like other questions. In fact, for a time printers used a different form of punctuation for rhetorical questions. It was an ordinary question mark turned around. That practice died out in the seventeenth century, but the point remains: rhetorical questions are different from other questions. They are asked more to produce an effect than to summon an answer.

The series of rhetorical questions Jesus asks about worry steers the listener to an answer that is obvious. But more: it is an obvious answer that worry has caused you to overlook. The cumulative effect of the questions is to challenge the validity of worry.

These are all rhetorical questions to which the answer is obvious, but it is significant that they are questions rather that statements. The answer to a rhetorical question may be obvious, but it is still an answer the listener provides. Even if the question is rhetorical, the listener is prompted to ask, "How do I respond to that question?" With a question, the listener is drawn into a dialogue, even if it is only an internal one. In this respect, a question engages the listener in a way a statement cannot. (Does that make sense?)

Jesus paints an evocative scene: Consider the lilies. Look at the wildflowers. Take a lesson from them. No gardener planted them. No one watered them. No one fretted over them. Yet God cared for them and supplied all that was needed. And look at them now, sprinkled across the field, dancing in the wind. Beautiful. Contented. Consider the lilies.

Then comes the question: Since God cares for them so magnificently, don't you think you can trust God to take care of you?

This passage is often embraced as among the most beautiful and comforting in all of Scripture.

But are these only words of comfort? Read another way they are words of challenge because they refuse to sanction our worry. E. Stanley Jones, a great missionary and author in the last century, famously declared, "Worry is atheism." The starkness of that statement is meant to arrest us. Jones went on to say that worry implies there is no God, or at least not a God who cares or a God who can act. Worry says, "It is all up to me." Worry sings, "I've got the whole world in my hands." It is the form of atheism that frets, "If I don't do it, it's not going to happen."

On one occasion, when Martin Luther was consumed with worry, his wife began to wear black. When Luther finally asked her why, she replied, "Haven't you heard? God is dead."

So when Jesus asks, "Why do you worry?" is he intending

to comfort us, or is he trying to challenge us or perhaps even rebuke us? It all depends on how we read the question. What inflection is used? You can ask the same question, using the very same words, but inflection can make it sound quite different and make it mean different things.

For instance, imagine you are tinkering with your child's bike, even though you have little aptitude for that sort of thing. Then your handyman neighbor saunters over and asks, "What are you doing?"

That question could be intended simply to start a conversation or as a way to segue to an offer of help.

But the neighbor could ask the question in a way that implies that obviously you do not know what you are doing: "What *are* you doing?" Asked in that way the question is a kind of rebuke.

Or, imagine you are mingling at a party and someone asks, "What's up with you?" The question could be nothing more than a casual conversation starter.

But what if that same question is accompanied by a shake of the head and a curled lip: "What's up with *you*?" It is the same question but with a very different implication.

So what is Jesus' intention when he asks, "Why do you worry?" If worry is a sign of a lack of faith, when Jesus asks, "Why do you worry?" that is not just a reassurance; it is also something of a rebuke.

One of the things I worry about is retirement. And because it is my worry, it seems entirely rational. I have known many pastors, including those in my own family, who have had difficulty with retirement, including the financial aspects. So I have done a lot of planning for retirement, and I have done my share of worrying about it, too. Jesus never says we should not think about the future or make provision for the future. After all, even the birds of the air—the very ones Jesus points to as examples of God's care—build nests and migrate to warmer climates in anticipation of colder weather. What Jesus rebukes is not the planning, but the worry. And, in regard to retirement, I have done a bit of both.

A while back I wrote a book with two other pastors about changes that are taking place in church life these days. The three of us were asked to address a gathering of pastors in Florida on the themes of the book.

After the second of my two definitive lectures on the state of the contemporary church, I sat down for lunch with a group of retired African American pastors. They were reminiscing about their early years in ministry—before the highways came through their part of rural Florida, before there was any money.

One pastor told about how the roof of his church had a big leak right over the pulpit. There was no money to repair the roof, so whenever it rained the ushers hustled to move the pulpit to one side so worship could proceed. Everyone at the table laughed (everyone, that is, except me—I was still trying to imagine the scene).

Another pastor told about how he was paid in chicken and beans when the church treasury ran out of funds. There were nods of recognition around the table.

Still another added, "That was a regular occurrence around our place. But one time when the church had no money, the members brought so much food to our house our children thought we never had it so good."

A lot of laughter accompanied those stories and some testimonies as well. "But we never wanted for anything." "Yes, God is good." "All the time, all the time." "The children never went to bed hungry."

After a time, I asked, "How about now, in retirement?" Everyone paused, as if trying to understand the question before responding. Eventually, one of the older pastors at the table gave me a bit of a smile and said, "It's the same God."

And I thought I had gone to Florida to give a lecture.

> "Consider the lilies of the field, how they
> grow: they neither toil nor spin, yet I tell you,
> even Solomon in all his glory was not arrayed
> like one of these. But if God so clothes the
> grass of the field, which today is alive and to-
> morrow is thrown into the oven, will God not
> much more clothe you, O you of little faith?"

It is strange that I would have to go all the way to Florida to see a lily. It was an inspiring sight, to be sure, but also something of a rebuke as well. "Lovely lilies," said Martin Luther, "how you rebuke our foolish nervousness."

CHAPTER 6

QUESTIONS ABOUT
THE REACH OF LOVE

✦✦✦✦✦✦✦✦✦

WE NOW TAKE UP SOME OF THE MOST CHALLENGING and radical questions Jesus asked, questions about the reach of love.

A lawyer asks Jesus, "Teacher, what must I do to gain eternal life?" (Luke 10:25-37). Jesus responds characteristically by asking a couple of questions of his own in return: "What is written in the Law? How do you interpret it?" These are softball questions. No particular challenge here. The lawyer answers them easily: "You must love the Lord your God with all your heart, with all your being, with all your strength, and with all your mind, and love your neighbor as yourself."

Jesus commends the lawyer for his answer, but the lawyer cannot leave well enough alone. He asks a follow-up question, "And who is my neighbor?" It is a lawyer's question. He is seeking a definition of terms. He is asking, in essence, "Who am I obliged to love? My family members? Those who live in my community? Those who believe the same things I do?" It is a question about the reach of love. If it were a sincere and open-ended question, Jesus might have been able to respond in a straightforward manner. But Luke indicates that the lawyer asks the question "to justify himself." In other words, he wants to be told that he is already doing it right. He wants to defend his conviction that there are limits to the command to love one's neighbor so that he can go on living as he has.

So in response Jesus tells a parable, commonly known as the parable of the good Samaritan. Parables are particularly good at sneaking past the conscious defenses of our own point of view and behavior. A parable insinuates itself. The late Clarence Jordan (Georgia peanut farmer, social activist, Greek scholar—yes, he was all those things) pointed out that a parable functions like the Trojan horse. It is so alluring that you let it into the inner court, unaware of the danger it contains. By the time you realize it should be defended against, it is too late. A parable can be captivating in the most literal sense of the word.

People are often drawn into stories of violence and heroism. So Jesus begins his parable by saying that a man going from Jerusalem to Jericho was ambushed by robbers, beaten, and left for dead. A priest and then a Levite—both religious leaders who served in the Temple—come upon the injured man and both pass by on the other side of the road. In other words, the very people one might expect to help do not. But then along comes a Samaritan—that is, a member of a despised group—who not only stops to help but also then puts the injured man on his own donkey, takes him to a safe place, and pays for his treatment.

The Trojan horse has gotten past the defenses of the law-yer, only waiting for the captivating question to complete the conquest: "What do you think? Which one of these three was a neighbor to the man who encountered thieves?" Game over. Checkmate. After the parable, there can be only one answer to Jesus' question, and the lawyer serves it up: "The one who showed him mercy."

One summer early in my ministry I attempted to act out this parable with a group of children during the church school hour. We gave it a decidedly modern twist. I parked my car on the shoulder of the road about a quarter of a mile from the church to give the impression it was disabled. That was not particularly difficult, given the condition of the car. It man-aged to look disabled even when it was barreling down the highway.

But just to be sure passersby would not miss the point, I lifted the hood of the car and even jacked it up for emphasis. Most of the children were hiding behind bushes in a nearby field, clutching flowers and cards that said, "Thank you. You are a good Samaritan," waiting for people to stop so they could leap from the bushes and shower these gifts of appreciation upon the good souls who stopped. I remember telling them not to give all the flowers and cards to the first person who stopped so we would have enough for the next roadside Samaritan.

I kept two children with me by the car. I chose these two because, although most children are accomplished at turning on a pathetic look at a moment's notice, these two clearly were masters.

We took our places. When a car passed I peered under

the hood and tried to look perplexed—which was not difficult, given my ignorance of anything mechanical—and the two children with me tried to catch the eye of the person driving the passing car with their most masterfully pathetic look.

To my surprise, car after car passed without stopping. A few slowed down but then proceeded on their way. The children behind the bushes began to become restless, complaining loudly that they were being torn apart by thorns and also complaining that they were getting their good shoes muddy. The two children who were with me added looks of boredom and impatience to pathetic on their facial pallets. I began to wonder how I could salvage some lesson for the children in this unexpected turn of events.

Then, when the worship hour was almost over and we were about to head back to the church, a station wagon slowed down a bit when it got to us. I was hopeful for an instant, then discouraged as it seemed to pass by like all the others. But then the car pulled over about fifty yards down the road and began to back up. The children in the bushes were suddenly quiet, waiting to pounce with thanksgiving.

A woman I did not recognize got out of the car and said, "Tim! What's going on?" and one of the children beside me replied, "Mom!" It seems she had just finished her shopping and was heading back to the church to pick up her son from church school when she spotted him beside this disabled car.

Tim hugged his mother, and the children appeared from the bushes with exultant cheers and surrounded them both as if they were celebrities from whom they wanted an autograph. The children gave Tim's mother every bouquet and a stack of cards. I introduced myself and explained what we were up to and thanked her for stopping. She held the flowers in her arms as if she had just been crowned the winner of a beauty pageant.

I still remember the sight of Tim and his mother driving away, their station wagon so full of flowers that it might have resembled a hearse—that is, if both of them had not been beaming, so obviously delighted with the events of the morning.

On the walk home it was obvious that all the children were pleased as well. Their voices cascaded with excitement. They beamed like fishermen who had caught a fish fit for a trophy on the last cast of the day.

If I recall correctly, I was able to extract a rather meager lesson from our experience, something about the importance of helping those in need. I did not have the heart to tell them that what happened that morning was precisely not what the parable of the good Samaritan intends to teach. It is not about helping members of one's own family, nor is it about coming to the aid of others we know.

In short, a mother helping her child in distress does not expect to receive a bouquet.

The reason the Samaritan is singled out in the parable is not because he helped the traveler by the side of the road. He is singled out because he is the least likely one to have done such a thing. In Jesus' day, Samaritans and Jews did not have anything to do with one another. They lived separately, believed different things. They were bitter enemies. So, normally, if a Samaritan saw a Jew beaten and bleeding by the side of the road, that would have been occasion for some satisfaction. Among all those who saw the injured Jew, the Samaritan has the best reason of all to say, "What has that to do with me?" But this Samaritan does not see a foreigner or a stranger or an enemy. This Samaritan sees a neighbor.

It is such a radical notion that we often lose our grip on its implications.

During a recent snowstorm, I came upon someone I know who was walking from the train station to his home. I pulled over to give him a ride. As he shivered inside the car, he said, "Thanks, you are a good Samaritan." I simply accepted his word of thanks. But I did think something along the lines of, "If you help only those who help you, what makes that worthy of note? Wouldn't the members of the Taliban do the same?"

Good Samaritan Hospital in the Boston area has this motto: "World class medical care, from our family to yours." The motto implies a certain familiarity and ease befitting a relationship between peers: "We'll take care of you because our families are friends." That is quite different from the hospital's namesake, the Samaritan who is singled out in the parable for going to great lengths to help a stranger.

For the most part, no one needs to be told to care for the basic needs of our families and friends. We do so almost by instinct. And, obviously, that is a good thing. But, as Jesus asked in another context, "If you love those who love you, what credit is that to you? For even sinners love those who love them. If you do good to those who do good to you, what credit is that to you? For even sinners do the same" (Luke 6:32-34). These questions also ask about the reach of love. They are rhetorical questions, of course, designed to imply an answer. And they are among the most challenging questions Jesus asked.

When Lloyd Van Vactor was kidnapped, these questions were brought home. I was new to ministry at the time and serving as Associate Minister at Saugatuck Congregational Church in Westport, Connecticut, a position Lloyd had once held. Lloyd had gone to the Philippines as a missionary of the United Church of Christ with his wife, Maisie, and their two young sons. Because of his long-standing relationship with our congregation, Lloyd was adopted as a special kind of missionary from our church. By the time I came to the church, in the late 1970s, Lloyd and Maisie were halfway around the world, but many in the congregation kept in touch through a regular exchange of letters. Most years Lloyd and Maisie would come to Westport on their annual trip back to the States. On some of those trips Lloyd would preach at the church, which was always a highlight of our year. Lloyd was tall and walked with long, lopping steps. His voice was as rich and smooth as melted butter, and his gentle manner was calming, even on first meeting.

Each year our church held an enormous fundraising event to support Lloyd's ministry—a pig roast and barbeque for the community that attracted droves of church members and other assorted carnivores to the church lawn. It was billed as a "Missionary Roast." Just to be sure no one missed the joke, to publicize the event each year, a large sign was put on the church lawn; it featured a cartoon of a missionary in somber clothes and a black Pilgrim hat, sitting in an enormous black pot with a fire under it. It was an attempt to be whimsical, of course. Today, in retrospect, it seems in bad taste, but at the time people loved that sign—that is, until harrowing events intruded.

Lloyd was far from the caricature of the missionary depict-
ed on the sign. He had gone to the Philippines to assume the
presidency of Dansalan College in the small city of Marawi.
The primary goal of the college is to educate the people of that
country, but a strong and explicitly stated secondary goal is to
improve the relationship between Christians and Muslims in
the Philippines by bringing together, as classmates, the future
leaders of both religions. This was an ambitious goal because
there have been four centuries of hostility between Muslims
and Christians in Marawi and the surrounding area. Violence
was common. Although Lloyd had achieved great success in
improving the interreligious understanding within the college,
the hostilities in the surrounding communities remained intense. When violence interrupted, Dansalan was a frequent
target.

On the evening of March 9, 1979, eleven armed men spir-
ited Lloyd from his office. The next day our church was in-
formed he had been kidnapped by members of a Muslim sect
and was being held for ransom. The senior minister immediately wrote a letter to tell the members of the congregation. He
passed along what little information he had and then added,
"Pray for Lloyd in his captivity. Pray for his wife, Maisie, as
she anxiously awaits word. Pray for both the Christian and
Muslim communities in the Philippines, that the violence
might stop. And pray for Lloyd's captors, that they might know
the peace of God."

I remember so clearly how word of Lloyd's captivity affect-
ed our entire church, and especially I remember the reaction
to that last request in the letter, the request for prayers for

Lloyd's captors and persecutors. It sent a strong and imme-
diate jolt through the congregation. Some church members
asked, with no small measure of exasperation, "Why should
we pray for them? They are threatening our friend." Others
said things like, "Sure, I'll pray for his captors. I'll pray that
they come to their senses. And then I'll pray that they get the
punishment they deserve."

Obviously, we did not need to be told to pray for Lloyd or
Maisie. Our prayers turn easily to the ones we love. We have
great concern for them. We want good things for them.

And it may not be too difficult to pray for Christians and
Muslims generally because such words as *Christian* and *Muslim* can seem comfortably vague. They can lack a human face.
The easiest prayers are always the most general. It is when our
prayers gain in specificity that they can gain in discomfort. So
it is not surprising that it was the last request in the letter that
many found so difficult. It was a request to extend the reach of
love beyond where we are used to taking it.

While Lloyd was being held captive, we received word
that Maisie had died, news that, in his captivity, he had not
yet heard. Naturally, news of Maisie's death only increased
the anger and resentment that Lloyd's friends felt toward his
captors. To be separated by death is one thing—people do
die, after all—but to be forcibly separated at the time of death
seemed cruel in the extreme. Nevertheless, the members of
our congregation did turn their anger into something construc-
tive. We started a memorial scholarship fund in Maisie's name
for American women who might want to pursue the ministry or
social work, as she had done.

✦✦✦✦✦✦✦✦✦

Embedded in this question is an answer that is unsettlingly clear: "If you love only those who love you, what credit is that to you?" Yes, exactly.

After twenty days Lloyd was released, as quickly and inexplicably as he had been abducted. His kidnappers didn't receive the ransom money that had been collected for his release. In the weeks after Lloyd's release, a question arose about how the money that was intended for his ransom should be spent.

Lloyd was given the choice as to how the funds would be used. He, too, decided to give the money for a scholarship fund, but the fund was not to be used for American students. Rather, the fund he established was very specifically earmarked for Dansalan College students who are part of the very Muslim sect that kidnapped him and threatened his life for those tormenting weeks of his captivity.

Even all these years later, his decision still astonishes me. Our congregation decided to help a beloved one of ours. Lloyd decided to give aid to his enemies. Jesus asks, "If you love only those who love you, what credit is that to you?" Jesus asks me that, and now Lloyd asks me, too; and although I have suggested that Jesus is not in the business of answers, embedded in this question is an answer that is unsettlingly clear: "If you love only those who love you, what credit is that to you?" Yes, exactly.

CHAPTER 7

QUESTIONS ABOUT HEALING

❖❖❖❖❖❖❖❖❖

THE HEALING ARTS BEGIN WITH THE practice of asking questions.

Even with all of the sophisticated tools available to practitioners of modern medicine, the healing process still begins with asking questions:

"What is your name?"

"How long has this been happening?

"Has this ever happened before?"

"Are you in any pain?"

"What letters do you see when you look at this chart on the wall?"

These questions, and ones like them, are straightforward—some are even quite routine—but they are essential to proper diagnosis and treatment.

In his time Jesus was known for being a healer as much as he was known for being a teacher. One of the titles given to Jesus is the Great Physician. The Gospels are filled with examples of Jesus healing every manner of disease. Such healings are called miracles—a word that means "signs." Such healings are signs that point to God. They are signs of God's presence and power.

It is not coincidence that the Great Physician is also the Great Questioner because healing begins with questions. Some of the questions Jesus asks sound very much like the questions of a modern physician.

When Jesus meets a man who is tormented by demons, he begins by asking the kind of question a physician would ask when first meeting a patient: "What is your name?"

When a father brings his son to Jesus, the boy is convulsed with a seizure. Jesus asks the question a physician would ask to aid his diagnosis: "How long has this been going on?"

When a blind man begs Jesus to restore his sight, Jesus applies a salve of saliva to the man's eyes and then, like a physician removing bandages after eye surgery, asks the man, "Do you see anything?"

Not all questions asked by practitioners of the healing arts are so straightforward and routine. Some questions dip deep into the mystery of how the human and the divine can join as a force for healing. Such was the question my own doctor asked.

A few years back I landed in the hospital after what I call "my unfortunate little episode." The medical term is atrial fibrillation, a condition characterized by a rapid and irregular heartbeat. If a regular heartbeat resembles the strong and steady beat of a Sousa march in 4/4 time, a heart beating to the tune of atrial fibrillation is more like the syncopated beat of reggae.

One doctor after another parted the curtains around my

bed and stood over me, asking the kind of questions you would expect under the circumstances:

"How long have you had these symptoms?"

"Is this the first time you have experienced this?"

"Are you allergic to any medications?"

Sometime later that day, my heart resumed its normal rhythm, as suddenly as it had been thrown out of whack. Under most circumstances, I would prefer to listen to reggae rather than the steady, boring beat of a marching band. When it comes to my heart, however, a steady beat is not boring. It is a great relief.

The next week I went for a follow-up appointment with my doctor. He is competent and thorough, and as a charming bonus, he has a delightful Irish brogue. He also asks a lot of questions; some of them were basic, like the questions I was asked in the hospital, but others were more searching. That was particularly the case on this day. My doctor was brimming with questions. Without looking up from a thick stack of records that had been taken in the hospital, chronicling my unfortunate little episode, he asked one question after another. He inquired about my own medical history, as well as the medical history of my family. He asked about my eating, drinking, and exercise habits, questions I rather awkwardly answered, knowing that my answers were not in every instance what he would want to hear.

Then he asked, "Do you experience stress in your life?" and I responded, "Well, sure." (I wanted to ask a question of my own: "Doesn't everybody?") He followed up, "At home or in your work?"

"Not so much at home. But in my work, sure."

Then he asked, "How can caring for souls be stressful?"

What a lovely description of ministry. If I could only spend more of my time "caring for souls," as he put it, that would be wonderful. But what sometimes keeps me up at night, wrestling with the angel (or with demons), are all those things that don't fit so neatly under the category of caring for souls: the board meeting that didn't go well, the budget shortfall, the parishioner who is angry with me, or the church leaders who are in conflict. Of course, I know that all of those things—and, indeed, everything I do as a pastor—are interpreted as caring for souls, at least indirectly. But sometimes it doesn't feel that way. So I simply replied, "Well, there's a lot involved in my work that doesn't always seem like caring for souls."

After a few more questions, he finally closed my thick file. With his elbows on the file in his lap, he leaned forward and, for the first time that visit, looked me straight in the eye. He said, "Here's the most important question: are you praying?"

At first I was a bit taken aback by the question, but I was also grateful that, finally, there was a question I could answer without feeling self-conscious or inadequate. "Why, yes, I pray every day." But he was not finished with this line of questioning: "Half an hour every day, uninterrupted, no distractions?"

I felt like I was looking for a place to hide. "Uh...well, uh...hmm...not exactly. Not every day, at least." Without shifting his gaze—he wasn't about to give me any wiggle room—finally he moved away from questions and offered his first statement: "It's the most important thing. For some people I might suggest meditation, but for you it's prayer."

Was he giving me spiritual advice or medical advice? Of

course, the answer is both. The spiritual and the physical are not two separate realms. My doctor's question—"Are you praying?"—implies that a spiritual practice can have medical benefits.

In the Bible there is no neat division between the spiritual and the physical. We are not bodies with spirits—not like "a ghost in a machine," as one philosopher put it. Instead, we are whole beings. And so there is no strict isolation of spiritual and physical illness. In such a worldview, there is no way to treat the body without treating the spirit, for body and spirit cannot be divided. The implication is that, if body and spirit are inextricably one, then spiritual practices like prayer can play a role even in the healing of the body. That understanding was implicit in my doctor's question: "Are you praying?"

I was a bit taken aback by his question, not only because it challenged me but also because it is not the kind of prescription I am used to getting from a doctor.

With the advent of modern medicine, we began to understand more about how the body works. Previously unexplained mysteries of the body came to be understood. Through modern medicine, we also learned how to intervene in bodily processes to stem disease, advance recovery, even hold death at bay, however temporarily.

Through this progress in science, and the attitudes it engendered, the body came to be viewed more or less in isolation. There developed a tendency in modern medicine to treat the body as a mechanism—a complex mechanism, certainly, but a mere mechanism nonetheless. There are parts of the body that may need to be repaired, others that must be replaced, and chemical treatments that are required. And, of course, many wonderful benefits have been achieved through this process.

Yet something else happened in the modern era through this process: the spiritual and the physical came to be understood—and treated—separately.

This modern division of spirit and body never completely prevented mystery from appearing in the realm of science, even in the most modern clinical settings. Most doctors I know can share stories of unexplained remission of a deadly disease. Taking placebos—often just simple sugar pills—can sometimes help a person recover from serious illness, presumably because the patient taking the placebo is convinced it will help. Doctors generally concede that a patient's positive attitude can greatly aid in recovery and that when a person has a strong will to live, sometimes death itself can be delayed— hardly something one would say about a mere mechanism.

My doctor clearly believes that there is no neat division between the spiritual and the physical. So he gave me two prescriptions. One was for a pill I was to take every night. The other was for thirty minutes of prayer every day, uninterrupted, with no distractions.

If our inner spiritual resources can help us fight disease, it makes sense to me that Jesus, who lived in unique spiritual communion with God, was able to help those around him tap those resources. His healings were not magic tricks. In doing a magic trick, if you say the right words and offer the right gestures, you can pull a rabbit out of the hat every time. Even Jesus was not able to heal all who came to him. Jesus' healings did not follow a formula. Instead, they point to the mysterious ways in which the human and the divine can collaborate in ways that result in healing.

The healings recorded in the Gospels are highly relational. They are made possible by the relationship between a human being and a divine being. So when Jesus encounters a man who has been paralyzed for thirty-eight years, he asks, "Do you want to get well?" That might sound like a silly question to ask someone who has been unable to walk for thirty-eight years. Of course, he wants to get well. Does Jesus need to ask? But Jesus is asking for more than mere information here. His question is a way of inviting the man into a healing partnership.

When my doctor asked, "Are you praying?" it was his way of saying that I need to invite the divine into a healing partnership with me. By asking, "Do you want to get well?" Jesus is inviting the man to bring himself into a healing partnership with Jesus. The paralyzed man is not an inanimate object. He is a person. He has a will. So Jesus' question might be rephrased, "Are you willing to work with me here?"

When a blind man cries out to Jesus on the road to Jericho, Jesus responds by asking him, "What do you want me to do for you?"

Is that just another silly question? If you are blind, of course what you want most of all is to have your sight restored. Why does Jesus have to ask?

Most of us have a tendency to assume that we know what another person needs or wants, particularly if that person is dealing with some kind of challenge or disability. But perhaps what the blind man wants, more than anything else in the world, is something other than the restoration of his sight. He might respond to Jesus' question by saying, "What I most want is to be reconciled with my father." Or, "I want to be able to share my life with someone." One of those, or something else entirely, might be his deepest yearning. You will never know unless you ask.

So when Jesus asks, "What do you want me to do for you?" he is showing respect for the man. He is not presuming to know what he wants. He is asking. And he is listening. It is a way of recognizing that the blind man is not defined by his disability. Jesus' question is a way of relating to the man as a human being. It is also his way of inviting him into a healing relationship.

Jesus asks the same question when he comes upon a blind beggar named Bartimaeus. Bartimaeus shouts at the top of his lungs, "Jesus, Son of David, show me mercy!" *Son of David* is one of the titles associated with the Messiah. Bartimaeus wants Jesus to know that, even though he is blind, he sees Jesus for who he is. He is making such a racket that the people around him try to shut him up. But Bartimaeus keeps shouting his plea—each time with more volume and more urgency. Hearing his name called, Jesus stops, stands still, and says, "Call him forward." So Bartimaeus immediately throws off his cloak—I picture him as a basketball player ripping off a warm-up suit when he has been called into the game—and runs to Jesus. He is probably panting a bit

So when Jesus asks, "What do you want me to do for you?" he is showing respect for the man. He is not presuming to know what he wants. He is asking. And he is listening.

when he hears Jesus ask him, "What do you want me to do for you?"

Bartimaeus, the one who already sees that Jesus is the Messiah, asks only for the gift of sight. Jesus says in response, "Go, your faith has healed you." And, sure enough, Bartimaeus's sight is restored and he follows Jesus. The healing partnership turns into a relationship between teacher and disciple.

"What do you want me to do for you?" A friend who used to direct shows for television tells me that a variation of this question is in almost every script. Sooner or later a character will ask of another, "What do you want?" He calls it the "ultimate question" because it gets to the crux of things. Often a story pivots on that question and how it is answered. It is common for such an exchange to be the turning point of a story.

Apparently, it is one of Jesus' favorite questions as well because he repeats it in a variety of circumstances. It is striking that this would be one of Jesus' favorite questions because one might expect that the savior of the world would more likely ask, "Do you want to know what you can do for me?" After all, those in positions of power are used to being served. It is another instance of Jesus upending the usual order of things. He is forever inviting those at the back of the line to come to the front of the line. In his realm the most exalted position of all is the role of servant. So it is not surprising that Jesus asks the servant's question: "What do you want me to do for you?"

CHAPTER 8

A QUESTION ABOUT ABUNDANCE

✦✦✦✦✦✦✦✦✦

IT IS AN INTENSE TIME FOR JESUS, with many demands on him and his disciples. Jesus' reputation as a teacher and healer has grown to such an extent that they are constantly surrounded and pressed by people who need something from him—a word from his mouth, a healing touch from his hand. Always something. (Mark 6:31-44)

Jesus can see the disciples are exhausted, so he says to them, "Let's get you a bit of a break in a quiet place so you can rest for a while." It is not an unexpected suggestion. Jesus was a pastor who was always running away from his congregation. His times of intense engagement with people were in rhythm with times apart, either alone or with his closest friends. So Jesus and the disciples get into a boat to go to a place where they can have a moment to themselves. The people are so eager to see Jesus, however, that they walk or run or hobble along the shore. And there they all are waiting, like a huge welcoming committee, even as Jesus is getting out of the boat on the other side of the lake.

Jesus takes pity on them because, as Mark puts it, they look like sheep without a shepherd. Another image comes to mind: baby birds, with beaks open as wide as can be, waiting to be fed with the words from his mouth. So Jesus teaches them until it starts to get dark. The disciples were already tired, and now they are hungry, too. I picture them like my children used to be on Sunday mornings. Late in the fellowship hour after worship they had had enough of church and would tug on my coat and say, "Dad, are we ever going to leave?"

The disciples are something like that. They have had enough of church for a time. They just want to get out of there. They are able to mask their own needs by claiming to have great concern for the people. They say to Jesus, "This is a remote place and the people look awfully hungry. We should send them away so they can buy something to eat."

Jesus turns it right back to them: "You give them something to eat."

The disciples are dumbfounded. The people blanket the landscape as far as the eye can see. The disciples ask, in essence, "Even if we could find a deli open at this hour, do you expect us to have enough money to buy enough food for this crowd?"

Jesus again turns it back to them, this time with a question: "How much bread do you have?"

At this point the disciples might have concluded that Jesus is playing games with them. However much bread they have with them, certainly it will not be enough to satisfy the hunger of all these people. Nevertheless, they oblige Jesus. They check their pockets and pouches and come up with five loaves and two fish. It seems obvious to them that it is not nearly enough. "We only have five loaves and two fish. Look," they say as they turn their pockets inside out, "that's it. That's all there is."

Jesus then offers a blessing and tells the disciples to serve up the scraps as if they are a feast fit for a king.

In the end, not only is everyone fed but also, like at every good potluck supper, there are leftovers, enough to fill twelve baskets. What had seemed like meager pickings had become a feast for five thousand.

Whatever we conclude actually happened on that hillside that day, it was taken to be a miracle—a word that means, literally, a sign that points to God. Apparently, it made quite an impression. It is the only miracle story that appears in all four Gospels.

Two of the Gospel writers, however, may have concluded that this miracle did not make enough of an impression on the disciples. Both Matthew and Mark tell of a second miracle that is almost an exact repetition of the first, as if the disciples missed the miracle the first time so they need to have it repeated. In the second account, Jesus is again teaching a great throng, this time four thousand instead of five thousand (Matthew 15:32-39; Mark 8:1-9). Once again, Jesus suggests the disciples should feed them. Again, the disciples are incredulous: "How can one feed these people bread here in the desert?" Then Jesus responds with the same question he asked the first time: "How much bread do you have?"

The disciples are quite literal in their answers. The first time Jesus asks, "How much bread do you have?" the disciples answer, "Five loaves and two fish." The second time he asks the question, they respond, "Seven loaves and a few fish."

Jesus' question, however, is a much more searching one. I am quite sure he wasn't interested in a head count of fish. It really did not matter if there were five loaves or seven or two or two hundred. The answer Jesus was looking for was an expression of trust. He wanted to hear the word *enough* or *plenty*. *We have enough to go around. We have plenty to share.*

In other words, I think Jesus was looking for evidence that his followers had embraced what has been called a theology of abundance. This approach to life affirms that, through God's generosity, there is enough—and more than enough—to meet our needs. Old Testament scholar Walter Brueggemann writes that God created the world in "an orgy of fruitfulness, everything in its kind is to multiply the overflowing goodness that pours from God's creator spirit."[10] And God did not stop lavishing that kind of abundant goodness on creation. God continues to provide abundantly for God's people. Whether it is manna that appears in the wilderness to feed the people of Israel, or bread and fish that are multiplied in the desert to feed the followers

◆◆◆◆◆◆◆◆◆

I think Jesus was looking for evidence that his followers had embraced what has been called a theology of abundance. This approach to life affirms that, through God's generosity, there is enough—and more than enough—to meet our needs.

of Jesus, there is plenty to go around. There is enough, and more than enough. A theology of abundance is marked by trust and gratitude.

The disciples, however, are more inclined toward a theology of scarcity. They are quite sure that they do not have enough to meet the needs of the people. People who approach life this way are always sure that there is never enough, so out of fear and self-concern, they protect whatever they have. So the disciples turn their pockets inside out and say, "See, nothing here." To which Jesus replies, "Look again. There in the fold of your pocket is a crust of bread. Offer that. I will supply the rest."

Whenever I read the different biblical accounts of the feeding of the five thousand, I hear in Jesus' question—*How much bread do you have?*—a question about my own life, my own abundance, my own sense of scarcity. Sometimes the question seems like a welcome lens that allows me to truly see the abundance, even the superabundance, of my life. Indeed, I have more than enough—a comfortable house and a lovely vacation home, a table filled night after night with wonderful veal stew or baked salmon, even the time to prepare some of those meals myself. I so often take those things for granted. I so often barely see them at all. Sometimes I hear in Jesus' question a reminder to see them, to appreciate them, to revel in the abundance.

On other occasions, I hear the question and still all I see is scarcity. Not material scarcity, perhaps, but scarcity of time or of love or of patience. A friend younger than I am was diagnosed with stage IV cancer last week, and my reaction was not so much sorrow for him and his family as fear for myself—will I have enough time? When I hear Jesus asking me to survey what I have been given in terms of time, I am pierced by my own perception of scarcity.

Some interpreters have suggested that perhaps the people who gathered to be with Jesus on those occasions had brought their own food with them, but out of self-concern and fear they did not have enough, they hid it from others. They kept the scraps under their cloaks or in pouches. Then, according to this interpretation, when they saw Jesus offer them whatever meager scraps of food he had, the people were moved to a more generous impulse, reached into their cloaks and pouches, and shared whatever they had brought. And in so doing they found it was enough. It was more than enough.

This interpretation resembles the old Russian folktale about a soldier who comes to a village and asks for food. One by one, the people of the village turn him away because they do not believe they have enough to share. So the soldier says, "Have you ever had stone soup? I can make delicious soup from a stone." One of the villagers gives him a stone, and the soldier puts it in a pot of water and starts cooking his "stone soup."

Then he says, "This soup will be good, but do you know what could make it even better? A few carrots." And someone supplies the carrots. He goes on, "The best stone soup I have had usually includes a few potatoes." And someone con-

Perhaps Jesus did not want them merely to see the miracle but rather to take part in the miracle and in some way to be the miracle.

tributes the potatoes. The soldier, in his oblique way, keeps inviting more contributions to the soup, and the people respond. Eventually, it truly is a delicious soup, and the villagers all sit down to eat it together. And there is enough, perhaps even a bit more than enough, for everyone. Those who were afraid to share even a bit of food with the soldier when he first came into town, convinced as they were that there is not enough to go around, ended up enjoying a feast. Together they had discovered something like a theology of abundance.

I think there may be something to this "stone soup" interpretation of the multiplication of the loaves and fish, and not because it makes it more palatable to our modern sensibilities. I am not drawn to this interpretation because we live in a scientific age that is skeptical of anything supernatural. If God wanted to multiply loaves and fish—or even make those fish waltz in three-quarter time, for that matter—God could do that. And if the hungry people gathered on the hillside were nothing more than like an audience at a magic show, watching Jesus perform a miracle of multiplication, it would still be a miracle.

But would it be any less a miracle if the alternative explanation were true? Given the way self-concern and fear grip the human heart, would it be any less a sign of God's presence if, for once, people were able to trust in God's abundance?

If that is the real miracle, it is not just a miracle the people see Jesus perform; it is a miracle in which they take part. Perhaps Jesus did not want them merely to see the miracle but rather to take part in the miracle and in some way to be the miracle.

People are sometimes asked, in one form or another,

"What do you have that can be used to fulfill Christ's mission in the world? How much of your time? How much of your money? How many of your gifts?" In other words, it's the question Jesus asked the disciples: "How many loaves do you have?" The temptation for many of us is to look at what we have and say to Jesus, "Not much of anything, just a few scraps—five loaves, two fish, whatever—certainly not enough to do all you are asking me to do. Not enough. Sorry, not enough."

But Jesus says, in essence, "Just offer it. It is only when you offer what you have that everyone will be fed. It is enough. It is more than enough."

We tend to devalue small things. Jesus exalts small things: the pinch of yeast that leavens the whole loaf; the woman who gives two pennies as an offering that Jesus says is the largest offering of all because she gave from what little she had; the kingdom of God compared to the mustard seed, the smallest of all seeds, which grows to be a tree large enough that birds can call it home; that scrap of bread you brought with you to the hillside that is used to help feed five thousand, but only if you offer it. It starts with what is already in your pocket.

Habitat for Humanity, the Christian housing ministry, started out as a dream planted like a mustard seed in the mind of Millard Fuller. The Habitat concept was simple: homes would be built in partnership with the poor through volunteer labor and sold to the poor through no-interest loans. No tax money would be used. No large foundations would fund it. It would be achieved through the work of individual Christians and local churches.

I first met Millard Fuller in the late 1970s. I was in seminary, and Millard was touring churches in Connecticut with a box full of pamphlets in the trunk of his car, trying to stir up support for this new housing ministry he had just started. At that time Habitat was barely three years old, but already there were projects in three African countries and at eleven locations in the United States. Habitat received a lot of criticism at that time. Some people thought it was too meager a response to the enormous need for decent housing for God's people in need. They said we would never get anywhere building just one house at a time. They withheld their support, waiting for a response to the need for decent housing that would be on a larger scale. "A drop in the bucket," is the way they put it at the time.

Today, barely three decades later, there are Habitat for Humanity projects in thousands of locations in more than one hundred nations around the world. Over six hundred thousand families live in homes built by Habitat. In the United States, Habitat is the largest provider of housing outside the federal government.

One of the reasons the kingdom of God starts out small is so that we can all have a piece of the action. If the kingdom of God started out as something larger than a mustard seed or a few scraps of bread, we would be so intimidated by the enormity of the reality in which we are invited to share that we might not even get started.

That day when I met Millard Fuller, he told me that the goal of Habitat is to eliminate substandard housing worldwide. I smiled politely, not wanting to tell him what I thought of his grandiose dream. Then he said, "And Martin, I want you to help us do that, to eliminate substandard housing worldwide."

To that, I gave a nervous laugh, and Millard said, "Now, you don't have to do it all yourself. Maybe you could start some Saturday by getting a group from your church to help with the project that is getting started here in Connecticut. Could you do that?" Yes, I could do that. That sounded a whole lot easier than trying to organize a group from my church to eliminate substandard housing worldwide.

When Habitat for Humanity was still a young movement, I attended a meeting of people in the start-up phases of Habitat projects. One man asked Millard how much money you should have in the bank before starting to build your first house. The total cost? Half the total cost? Millard responded, "How much money do you need to start? How much money do you have in your pocket?"

Millard's question was essentially the same as Jesus' question: "How many loaves do you have?" Both questions challenge the listener to embrace a theology of abundance, to consider that you have enough—enough to share, enough to get started. What you have may seem small, but God can work with small things if we have the faith to offer them. You might even discover, in the end, that you not only have enough, you have more than enough. It was a feast you were carrying around in your pocket, all along.

Mother Teresa of Calcutta began her orphanage in that way. She told her superiors, "I have three pennies and a dream from God to build an orphanage."

Her superiors chided her: "You can't build an orphanage with three pennies.... With three pennies you can't do anything."

"I know," she said, with a sly smile, "but with God and three pennies I can do anything."

But the miracle of multiplication can be easily missed, even if it is reenacted repeatedly. In Mark's Gospel, the original twelve disciples are frequently getting it wrong. In a follow-up story to the multiplication of the loaves and fish, they seem particularly dense (Mark 8:14-21). They feasted on the miraculously multiplied loaves and fish—not once, but twice. After the second time this miracle is performed the apostles get in a boat with Jesus, but they forget to bring some of the leftovers with them, and they are hungry. Jesus seizes on the opportunity to make a point. He says, "Beware of the yeast of the Pharisees and the yeast of Herod." Here Jesus is using an analogy to warn the disciples not to seek nourishment from the teachings of the Pharisees or to follow Herod.

The disciples, who are in no frame of mind to pick up on Jesus' wordplay, look at one another and respond, "He said this because we have no bread."

Jesus, not even trying to hide his impatience at this point, fires a rapid round of questions, "Why are you talking about the fact that you don't have any bread? Don't you grasp what has happened? Don't you understand? Are your hearts so resistant to what God is doing? Don't you have eyes? Why can't you see? Don't you have ears? Why can't you hear? Don't you remember?"

It's then that we can see why Jesus is so annoyed, because he goes on to suggest that this is not the first time the disciples have been so dense. They have missed other things along the way. Jesus asks, "When I broke five loaves of bread for those

++++++++++

When Jesus asks, "How much bread do you have?" he is not asking for an inventory of available baked goods. He is asking for an inventory of the heart.

five thousand people, how many baskets full of leftovers did you gather?" They answer, "Twelve." "And when I broke seven loaves of bread for those four thousand people, how many baskets full of leftovers did you gather?" Still clueless, they reply, "Seven." With that response, Jesus has one more question for them: "And you still don't understand?"

Jesus had let them see a stunning glimpse of divine power, and all the disciples could perceive or remember was a picnic in the sun. The disciples had feasted on a miracle, but while their stomachs were still full, not a trace of the miracle was left in their hearts and minds. Obviously, a theology of scarcity is awfully hard to shake.

When Jesus asks, "How much bread do you have?" he is not asking for an inventory of available baked goods. He is asking for an inventory of the heart. You may see a few crumbs. Jesus sees a feast. Jesus' question is a challenge to trust his perception more than your own. The comfort in Jesus' question is in his confidence that, if you exhibit that kind of trust, the answer to his question is always, "Enough. More than enough."

CHAPTER 9

THE QUESTIONS JESUS ANSWERS

❖❖❖❖❖❖❖❖❖

LET'S REVIEW THE MATH. IN THE GOSPELS Jesus asks 307 questions. By contrast, he is asked only 183 questions. Most striking of all, Jesus gives direct answers to only eight of those 183 questions he is asked. It seems clear that Jesus prefers to be the one asking the questions. In fact, Jesus is more than forty times more likely to ask a question than to answer one directly.

If Jesus is asked a question, he is much more likely to give an indirect answer than a direct one. For every time Jesus answers a question directly, he responds indirectly more than twenty times. In other words, he is twenty times more likely to offer an indirect answer than a direct one. Although this is a book about the questions Jesus asks, in this chapter, we take up the manner in which Jesus answers questions. First, we will look at some of the ways Jesus offers indirect answers to the questions he is asked. Then, we will turn to the eight questions he answers directly.

Some of Jesus' indirect answers are in response to people who are trying to trap him with their questions. At one point, the Sadducees press Jesus for details about the nature of the afterlife (Mark 12:18-27). The Sadducees were a conservative Jewish sect that rejected the belief, growing within other segments of Judaism, that the dead would be raised at the end of history. So the Sadducees lay out a scenario in which they try to demonstrate the absurdity of any belief in a life after death. They remind Jesus that, according to the law of Moses, if a man dies, his next oldest brother is obligated to marry the widow. The Sadducees then go on to spell out a scenario in which one brother after another marries the widow and subsequently dies. (It does make you wonder if, as the pattern unfolded, the younger brothers might have been tempted to join the Foreign Legion, just to get out of town.) According to this scenario, in the end the widow had a total of seven husbands, all of whom died. Then she herself died. It's the one part of this ridiculous scenario that sounds realistic. She died after being married to and burying seven brothers? No kidding.

The Sadducees construct this implausible scenario to set up the question they ask Jesus: who would be her husband in the resurrection? To be sure, it is a thorny question. One bride for seven brothers? I would not want to moderate that family meeting.

Jesus begins his response by asking an exasperated question: "Isn't this the reason you are wrong, because you don't know either the scriptures or God's power?" (v. 24). Then, returning to the Sadducees' question, Jesus says, in essence, that it is only a sticky situation if we imagine our future life as being just like this life. But the afterlife will be different, unlike anything we have yet experienced. We will live like angels, Jesus says. But he does not answer the unspoken follow-up question: how do angels live? His answer is only implied: we cannot know.

The Pharisees, a group known for the way they scrupulously keep Jewish law, also try to trap Jesus with a question: "Does the Law allow people to pay taxes to Caesar or not?" (Matthew 22:15-22). If Jesus answers yes, he will be perceived as supporting the hated occupying Roman forces. If he answers no, he is in danger of stirring the ire of those same forces. Jesus, obviously irritated by the attempt to trap him, once again answers a question with a question: "Why do you test me, you hypocrites?" Then, pointing to a coin, he asks another question: "Whose image and inscription is this?" This is a pattern repeated throughout the Gospels: time and again, when Jesus is asked a question, his initial response is to offer a question of his own. When the Pharisees respond to Jesus' question by saying that it is the emperor's image on the coin, Jesus concludes his enigmatic answer: "Give to Caesar what belongs to Caesar and to God what belongs to God."

After Jesus is arrested he is brought before Pilate, the Roman governor of Judea. Pilate asks Jesus, "Are you the king of the Jews?" Pilate may not be trying to trap Jesus with the question. Rather, Pilate may be asking it on behalf of those who are. Among the Jews it would be considered heresy to make such a claim. So, in John's account of the encounter, Jesus tries to determine if someone put this question in Pilate's mind. He responds to Pilate's question with one of his own:

"Do you say this on your own or have others spoken to you about me?" (John 18:33-38). The other Gospels record that Jesus responds to Pilate's question by saying, "That's what you say" (Matthew 27:11-14; Mark 15:1-5; Luke 23:1-5). In each instance, Jesus avoids giving a direct answer. Matthew and Mark include the detail that Jesus responds to Pilate's follow-up questions with silence. That is, Jesus often avoids giving direct answers to questions, and sometimes he refuses to give any kind of answer at all.

In some instances, Jesus uses indirect answers as a teaching tool. When a lawyer asks Jesus, "Teacher, what must I do to gain eternal life?" (Luke 10:25-37), Jesus characteristically responds by asking a couple of questions of his own: "What is written in the Law? How do you interpret it?" The lawyer responds: "You must love the Lord your God with all your heart, with all your being, with all your strength, and with all your mind, and love your neighbor as yourself." Jesus affirms the lawyer's answer, but then the lawyer has an additional question: "And who is my neighbor?" Of course, Jesus could have answered that question directly, perhaps by saying something like, "Your neighbor is anyone in need." Instead, he responds to the question by telling the parable of the good Samaritan. In the parable, two respected religious figures come upon a man who has been beaten by robbers and lies bleeding by the side of the road. Neither one stops to help. But then a Samaritan stops to help. To those originally hearing the parable, it would be a surprise twist because in Jesus' day Samaritans and Jews would have nothing to do with one another. Jesus concludes his parable with a question: "What do you think? Which one of these three was a neighbor to the man who encountered thieves?" The lawyer responds, "The one who demonstrated mercy toward him." If Jesus had answered the question directly ("And who is my neighbor?"), the lawyer would have had Jesus' answer. By contrast, when Jesus responds to the question with the parable, the lawyer is enabled to discover his own answer. It is a tool employed by many of the best teachers.

Not all of Jesus' indirect answers are as helpful. For instance, when Jesus learns that his friend Lazarus is ill, Jesus is determined to go back to Judea to minister to him (John 11:1-16). The disciples are incredulous: "Rabbi, the Jews were just now trying to stone you, and are you going there again?" Jesus again responds with a question of his own, this time followed by what can only be described as a non sequitur: "Aren't there twelve hours in the day? Whoever walks in the day doesn't stumble because they see the light of the world. But whoever walks in the night does stumble because the light isn't in them." Huh? I can imagine the bemused disciples asking, "What does that have to do with anything, Jesus? Can we get back to our question?"

In the Gospels there are eight questions to which Jesus gives a direct answer. It is a small, and rather motley, amalgam of questions. So it would be difficult, if not impossible, to generalize about the nature of the questions Jesus chooses to answer directly.

Three of the questions Jesus answers directly have to do with his interpretation of the law. When Peter asks Jesus if he is required to forgive as many as seven times, Jesus responds, "Not just seven times, but rather as many as seventy-seven times" (Matthew 18:21-22). It may not be the answer Peter is looking for, but at least he gets a direct answer.

When some Pharisees ask Jesus if he agrees with Moses that a husband may divorce his wife for "any reason," Jesus responds, "I say to you that whoever divorces his wife, except for sexual unfaithfulness, and marries another woman commits adultery" (Matthew 19:3-9). The Pharisees may be trying to trap Jesus into contradicting Moses, but in this instance that does not prevent Jesus from giving a direct answer.

When a rich young man asks Jesus, "Teacher, what good thing must I do to have eternal life?" Jesus begins his response by asking another question in return, "Why do you ask me about what is good? There's only one who is good." But then Jesus immediately follows that response with a more direct answer: "If you want to enter eternal life, keep the commandments" (Matthew 19:16-22).

Jesus gives another direct answer in response to a question from the scribes: "Which commandment is the most important of all?" (Mark 12:28-34): "Jesus replied, 'The most important one is Israel, listen! Our God is the one Lord, and you must love the Lord your God with all your heart, with all your being, with all your mind, and with all your strength. The second is this, You will love your neighbor as yourself. No other commandment is greater than these.'"

Actually, at first reading this may not seem to qualify as a direct answer, because when Jesus is asked which is the greatest commandment, he does not simply offer one. Instead, he names two commandments. If Jesus were simply hedging bets here—like someone who, when asked to name his favorite flavor of ice cream, says he likes one scoop of vanilla and another of chocolate—then, perhaps, this would not qualify as a direct answer. But Jesus' answer here is both direct and nuanced. He is making the point that the commandments to love God and love neighbor are as inextricable as two steps of the same dance.

It may not be surprising that four—that is, half—of the questions Jesus answers directly are about the law. Direct questions about the law would seem to require direct answers. Nevertheless, as we have already seen, Jesus does not always give direct answers to questions about the law. When Jesus is asked if it is lawful to pay taxes to Caesar or what one must do to inherit eternal life, he responds indirectly (Matthew 22:15-22; Luke 10:29-37).

In Matthew's Gospel, there is an instance in which it seems as if Jesus is prodded into giving a direct answer out of raw exasperation. It occurs immediately after the Transfiguration, a momentous event in Jesus' life and in the experience of his closest friends (Matthew 17:1-13). Like many mountaintop experiences in the Bible, it takes place on a mountaintop. Jesus is there with his trusted inner circle—Peter, James, and John—when he is transfigured (that is, transformed) before their eyes. The awe-struck disciples see Jesus chatting with Moses and Elijah, both of whom were believed to be precursors of the Messiah. Then, just to be sure the disciples do not miss the point, out of a bright cloud they hear the voice of God, repeating what was said at Jesus' baptism: "This is my Son whom I dearly love. I am very pleased with him. Listen to him!" It is a turning point. Jesus' friends and followers begin to see him for who he is.

They might have preferred to linger, but no one can stay on a mountaintop forever. After spending time on a mountaintop, however, it is natural to want to bring some of the peak experience with you, to tuck it away in a place where it can be maintained for a time. Otherwise, the transition to the rest of life can be just too abrupt and jarring.

For Jesus and his small circle of disciples, however, the descent from the ecstasies of the mountaintop and the exigencies of the valley is anything but smooth (Matthew 17:14-21). As they are still coming down the mountain, they hear and see a roiling commotion. Soon they find themselves wading into a torrent of urgent need. A man has brought his epileptic son to be healed by Jesus, and in his absence, the disciples try to help as they have seen Jesus do on so many occasions, but to no avail. When Jesus hears about what has happened, he asks two exasperated questions. We can picture Jesus rolling his eyes and offering a sigh as he asks: "You faithless and crooked generation, how long will I be with you? How long will I put up with you?"

But then Jesus cures the boy instantly. Later, when they are alone, the disciples want to know why they were not able to wield the same healing power. Jesus gives an answer as direct as an arrow speeding to the bull's eye: "Because you have little faith."

It is as direct an answer as any Jesus gives. It is a response born out of the same exasperation as the questions that immediately preceded it. Perhaps that is not surprising. Elsewhere Jesus seems particularly impatient with the disciples' lack of faith. But could Jesus also be annoyed because he has been yanked off the mountaintop so abruptly?

When Jesus and his disciples approach Jerusalem, they ask him where he would like to eat the Passover meal (Mark 14:12-16). Obviously, this was a time before street signs and addresses, so Jesus' answer is necessarily quite detailed: "Go into the city. A man carrying a water jar will meet you. Follow him. Wherever he enters, say to the owner of the house, 'The teacher asks, "Where is my guest room where I can eat the Passover meal with my disciples?"'" He will show you a large room upstairs already furnished. Prepare for us there."

The instructions sound like they could be from a spy novel. Who is this mysterious man carrying a jar of water as a high sign, and where will he take them? The disciples are not told, and neither are we. So Jesus' answer is cloaked in some mystery, but it is a direct answer nonetheless.

Jesus is at table with his disciples when he announces that someone at that table will betray him (John 13:21-30). The disciples look around the table and cannot imagine that any of them would be the betrayer. Peter, who is next to Jesus, leans in and asks, "Lord, who is it?" Jesus does not offer a name, but he does give Peter a direct answer: "It's the one to whom I will give this piece of bread once I have dipped into the bowl." Then Jesus takes a piece of bread, dips it in the dish, and hands it Judas. The other disciples do not pick up on the significance of the gesture, and we are not told if Peter fully understands, either. Peter often is portrayed in the Gospels as being dense as a rock (which is the literal meaning of the name Peter). Nevertheless, Peter does get a direct answer to his question.

The last direct answer Jesus gives is in response to a

question that in other instances he seems determined to avoid. After his arrest, he is brought before a council consisting of the chief priests, elders, and scribes of the temple in Jerusalem (Mark 14:53-62). The high priest asks Jesus if he is the Messiah. Many times Jesus has avoided answering similar questions about his identity. For instance, earlier in Mark's Gospel, when Jesus asks his disciples, "Who do you say that I am?" and Peter responds, "You are the Christ," Jesus immediately gives them a stern order not to tell anyone that, indeed, he is the Christ, the Messiah (Mark 8:29-30). Also in Mark, often when Jesus performs a healing, he gives instructions to witnesses of the healing not to tell anyone about it, which is an effort to protect his identity. And when Pilate asks Jesus, "Are you the King of the Jews?" Jesus gives an indirect answer: "That's what you say" (Mark 15:1-5). By striking contrast, when Jesus is asked by the high priest of the temple, "Are you the Christ, the Son of the blessed one?" Jesus' answer is as direct and pointed as any he offers: "I am." In those two words is a claim as big as the universe. We can only imagine why Jesus is so direct in his answer. Perhaps it is because the time is short and, as one older member of my church used to say, "At my stage of life time is too short to waste on anything but the truth." Perhaps Jesus is simply annoyed by the goading and posturing of the temple officials and so he decides to let it rip. Whatever the reason, in this instance, Jesus offers a direct answer to the question that in some way is *the* question, and his answer is made all the more dramatic by its brevity.

✦✦✦✦✦✦✦✦✦

It is the questions Jesus asks that have particular power to engage us.

– 96 –

Well, that's it. That is the complete catalogue. Those are the eight questions to which Jesus offers a direct answer. From Jesus' answers we learn something about how he interprets the law, his understanding of the central role of faith is reinforced, and his identity as the Messiah is affirmed. It is striking to me, however, that if we only had Jesus' answers—and particularly if we only had his direct answers—we would be missing so much. We prefer direct answers from a mechanic who is repairing our car or from an accountant who is preparing our tax return or from a teenage son when he is asked, "What time did you get in last night?"

In other circumstances, however, direct answers are not enough. A teacher who aims to transform our lives needs more than direct answers. If the Gospels consisted mostly of people asking Jesus direct questions and Jesus providing direct answers, the narrative would be flattened and perhaps even something of a bore. In the end, an Answer Man Jesus is just not all that compelling.

Instead, it is the questions Jesus asks that have particular power to engage us, especially over time. Some of Jesus' questions are straightforward, but many more of Jesus' questions are more like his parables. There is more than one way to interpret them. We can see something different each time we encounter them. They are evocative—that is, able to evoke something in us. The questions have a power to move us, and often to a place we have not been before.

So, yes, it is important to consider the answers Jesus offers. But direct answers, at least, are not central to his teaching. Instead, it is the questions Jesus asks that are central, and it is to those questions we now return.

CHAPTER 10

QUESTIONS ABOUT
WHO JESUS IS

❖❖❖❖❖❖❖❖❖

SIMPLE QUESTIONS ARE OFTEN THE MOST DIFFICULT to answer,
and so it is with one of the questions Jesus asks. The question is raised while the disciples are with Jesus in Caesarea
Philippi (Mark 8:27-30). They have just left Galilee, where
they endured the constant presence of eager crowds and the
press of human need. Now they are in a place that is far from
the swelling crowds, and they have a chance to reflect and talk
with the inner circle.

The disciples are aware that there is a lot of speculation
going around about who Jesus is and who he isn't, and Jesus
himself seems just as glad to steer clear of the subject. Then,
in Caesarea Philippi, Jesus himself asks the question that had
been thickening the air: "Who do people say that I am?" The
disciples are able to answer that question with ease: "Some
say John the Baptist, but others Elijah, and still others Jeremi-
ah or one of the prophets," all people, Jewish tradition holds,
who will prepare the way for the coming Messiah.

Jesus then follows up that question with another: "But who

do you say that I am?" This question drops like a silver dollar on a slate floor. It is followed by the kind of silence that hangs in the air. No one seems to want to answer the question. I imagine some of the disciples casting down their eyes like students who are hoping and perhaps praying they will not be called on by the teacher. I also imagine other disciples looking at one another the way my parents looked at each other when I asked if there really is a Santa Claus, a desperate look that says, "Are you going to take this one or must I?"

Why is that question so difficult to answer? By this time, the disciples had already traveled many miles with Jesus. They had heard him preach. They had seen the lame walk and the blind blink their eyes with new sight after encountering Jesus. Certainly they must have already answered this question in the privacy of their own hearts. Why was it so difficult to give voice to their answer?

Well, we know, for instance, how difficult it can be to be the first to say, "I love you," to another. It is difficult to be the first to break the silence with such a large truth. One does not say something like that for the first time without sweaty palms and a dry mouth. We may hesitate, not because we doubt the words are true, but because, having spoken the truth, we can no longer ignore its implications for our lives.

Peter, never one to be shy, cracks open the silence: "You are the Christ, the Son of the living God." It took a lot of courage to say it. If it is true, it is enough to turn the world upside down and to shake everything loose. If it is not true, you can get yourself stoned to death as a blasphemer for saying it.

But Peter says it anyway, and in response, Jesus gives him

the only blessing he ever offered for a single individual. Jesus says, "Blessed are you, Simon son of Jonah," the kind of name used only on special occasions. Then Jesus goes back to calling him Simon Peter (that is, *the Rock*) and tells him he is the rock on which he intends to build his church. It is hard to imagine a higher honor. And what qualifies Peter for this honor is simply a blessed glimpse of the truth and a willingness to be the first finally to give it expression.

The other disciples are probably more than a little relieved to have it said at last and perhaps a bit grateful that they did not have to answer Jesus' question themselves. They can raise their eyes again because Peter has answered the question for them. Or so they think, because, of course, no one can answer such a question for another. Any who would be Jesus' disciples must eventually answer it for themselves.

The first question—"Who do people say that I am?"—is as easy for us as it was for the original twelve disciples. The answer is easily obtained. As famous baseball manager Casey Stengel used to say, "You could look it up." What do people say? To find out, we could conduct on-the-street interviews or go to a library and query the keenest minds of history or of our own time. We will find no shortage of answers.

Many theologians have offered their own answers: Karl Rahner described Jesus as "a perfected human person." John A. T. Robinson claimed Jesus was "the human face of God." Dietrich Bonhoeffer saw him as "the man for others." Many Latin American theologians view Jesus as the great liberator. Jürgen Moltmann referred to Jesus as "the crucified God." And you don't have to be a theologian to have your own answer. Bruce Barton, an American businessman turned author, said that Jesus was the greatest salesman who ever lived. The poet Swinburne's bitter lines refer to Jesus as "the pale Galilean," who has caused the world to grow gray from his breath. When my daughter was four years old, she referred to Jesus as "God's best friend."

"Who do people say that I am?" There is no lack of answers to that question. Just listen or read, and you will find more answers than anyone could possibly need. And you can answer a question like that without offending anyone. A question like that could be asked in the public schools and not jeopardize the separation of church and state. A student can safely answer that question historically or sociologically. It does not ask for commitment of any kind. A person can answer that question and still follow the cynic's creed: "Consider everything, commit to little, keep moving."

But then comes the second question: "Who do you say that I am?" Although only a single word in this question is different, that one word makes all the difference. The answer to this question is not found in the words of others or in the thousands of books about Jesus. This question is difficult because the answer is found so terribly close, as close as one's own heart. There is no escape into the comforts of objectivity. You cannot merely sit on the fence and describe what you see on both sides. You have to jump to one side or the other. This question demands not so much the insight of your mind as the allegiance of your life.

Although this question has been answered in countless ways in countless lives, C. S. Lewis contended that the possible answers are more limited than we might like to think. He concluded we have but two options:

> [My aim] is to prevent anyone from saying the really foolish thing people say about Him, such as "I'm ready to accept Jesus as a great moral teacher, but I don't accept His claim to be God." That is the sort of thing that we must not say. A man who was merely a man and said the sort of things Jesus said would not be a great moral teacher. He would either be a lunatic—on a level with the man who says he is a poached egg—or else he would be the Devil of Hell. You must make your choice. Either this man was, and is, the Son of God; or else a madman or something worse. You can shut Him up for a fool, you can spit on Him and kill Him as a demon; or you can fall at His feet and call him Lord and God.[11]

Many students prefer true-or-false questions on a test because, even if they have absolutely no idea which answer is correct, they still have an even chance of guessing correctly. But with a question like, "Who do you say that I am?" such an absolute either/or is uncomfortable. The options are too starkly presented, the choices too few. When faced with the need for decision, we are tempted to ask, "Don't you have any essay questions?" We want to be able to qualify our answers. We want to be able to say, "Yes, but on the other hand..."

It is common to hear the objection that in matters of faith

the language of decision is too confining to reflect the ambiguities of experience. Those who are uncomfortable with the language of decision often substitute words that emphasize evolutionary growth in their understanding of God and their relationship with Jesus. They employ images such as "pilgrimage" or "spiritual journey." Instead of arriving at a decision, they are perpetually en route. That is the posture assumed by many progressive Christians. We may not be ready to decide, but we are willing to grow.

Interpreters of the Christian religion sometimes emphasize the role of either decision or growth to the virtual exclusion of the other. Some focus on a particular time when they decided to "turn their lives over to Christ." They are concerned with the particular moment of conversion or commitment and often dismiss talk about growth and pilgrimage as vague and wishy-washy.

Others are unable to point to a moment of decision in their experience. If we have grown in our faith and commitment to Jesus, it has been by a slow, uneven process that is never quite complete. For the most part, we have put so much emphasis on the slow growth of faith that we run the danger of never putting forth the question, "But who do you say that I am?" We can be so concerned about distinguishing ourselves from so-called born-again Christians that we simply never get around to responding to the question. We view the idea of a once-and-for-all decision as a distant possibility, or we may reject the notion entirely as being too simplistic to reflect the vagaries and subtleties of our experience.

What is often lost in drawing such distinctions is that it

poses a false choice. Both decision and growth have a place in relationships, including in our relationship with Jesus. This is easy to observe in matters of the heart. There is a place for the slow flowering of a love, but there is also a place for the decision to marry. We may not be able to decide to love someone, but we can decide to commit ourselves to the one we have begun to love. Further, we may find that our commitment to another allows our love for that person to increase as nothing else can. In a similar way, in our relationship with Jesus it is important to recognize that there is a place for the slow growth of belief, but it is equally important to grant the place of decision. Here, too, growth and decision are not unrelated. It can be in living out the implications of our commitment to Jesus that our faith in him can ripen and flourish.

Obviously, the question, "But who do you say that I am?" presses the moment of decision. Jesus himself seemed to recognize how difficult the question is. After all, he does not ask it of the disciples until after they had traveled many miles together, not until after they had already seen lives changed with a mere word from his lips or a touch of his hand. And even after that the disciples do not feel fully prepared to answer such a question. One never does.

Perhaps we tend toward more general talk about God because we cannot bring ourselves to believe the peculiar notion that God was—and somehow still is—uniquely present in a common first-century Jew. But often the opposite is the case. Our uneasiness with Jesus may not derive from our doubt that God was in Jesus in a unique way. Rather, our uneasiness may flow from our suspicion that it may be true, after all. And if it is true, then we must confront God and confront ourselves more fully. Who feels entirely ready for that?

A few years ago, I had a memorable dinner with four ministers, one of whom was Frederick Buechner, a noted novelist who is also a Presbyterian minister. As we were lingering over coffee and dessert, I posed this question to the group: "If you could meet anyone in history, who would it be?" Responses varied. As I recall, I said I would want to meet the Apostle Paul. When we had all had a chance to respond to the question, I pointed out the curious fact that, among these four Christian ministers, no one said that he would want to see Jesus. Fred immediately responded, "No. Oh, no. I would dissolve into a puddle of tears."

I know what he was talking about. Jesus brings the presence of God to me in such a powerfully intimate way that I feel uncommonly vulnerable, in ways that all the talk about God in more general terms does not.

And yet, the question is still discomforting. Perhaps it embarrasses us because we are not sure of the answer or because we are not sure we want to speak aloud what we are certain of.

Our uneasiness with Jesus may not derive from our doubt that God was in Jesus in a unique way. Rather, our uneasiness may flow from our suspicion that it may be true, after all.

There is no one right answer to that question (though there are probably some wrong answers). But all of the true answers have some real consequences for our lives, I think. Is Jesus a teacher? What would it mean to live as his student? Is Jesus the one who makes peace possible in the world? How can I live into his peace? Is Jesus a man arrested and put to death by the state? What does following him mean for Americans, who have the highest incarceration rate of any country in the world?

When Michael Greene, a British historian of evangelism, addressed a gathering of United Church of Christ ministers a number of years ago, he sparked lively debate by defining evangelism as "chatting about Jesus" and by asking us, "When was the last time you told your congregation what Jesus means to you?" At the hotel bar afterward, Greene's remarks sparked a lively exchange. Many felt that Greene's question was dangerously simplistic, smacked of fundamentalism, and represented the kind of piety they had hoped to escape by joining a liberal denomination like the United Church of Christ.

I was among those who felt that Greene's question was a challenging and appropriate one. In fact, I was haunted by it. I could not answer it with certainty. As a Christian preacher I talk about Jesus a good deal, but talking about is quite different from expressing devotion. It is the difference between talking about a loved one and sending a love letter.

Greene's question was still in my mind when I preached for the last time to my congregation of nine years, First Congregational Church (United Church of Christ) in Burlington, Vermont. I spent almost the entire sermon speaking devotionally about Jesus, which would be about as unremarkable in some traditions as it was startling in my own. The sermon was an attempt to answer Jesus' question, "But who do you say that I am?" Here is how I concluded that sermon, which I entitled, "What It's All About":

As I am about to leave, there is something I
want to tell you. I want to tell you what Jesus
means to me. I want to share my belief that
everything depends on him. I want to urge you
to learn from him. I want to assure you that
you can lean on him in times of trouble. I want
to ask you to listen to his words of challenge.
I want to tell you that I believe that you can
entrust your life to him. I want to affirm that
he is Lord of this church and that in his name
you are freed to love one another and empow-
ered to share that love with a hurting world. I
want to profess that, though once people could
not look at the face of God and live, now we
are invited to look at the face of God in him,
in Jesus, and live as we have never lived before. He is Emmanuel, God with us, God with
us all, whether we are together or apart. That's
what it's all about. That's all I know. Amen.

At the conclusion of that sermon I stood at the door and
shook hands with the members of the congregation for the last
time as their pastor. One woman, a beloved saint of the church,
came to the head of the line but was so overcome with emotion
that she could not speak and went to the back of the line. I
assumed she simply did not know how to say good-bye. When
she finally reached me again, she extended her hand to shake
mine, her shockingly blue eyes magnified by tears. Her voice
cracked as she asked, "Why didn't you tell us this before?"

I did not know how to respond. And now it is her question
that haunts me.

CHAPTER 11

A QUESTION FROM THE CROSS

✦✦✦✦✦✦✦✦✦

ACCORDING TO BOTH MATTHEW AND MARK, the last words Jesus speaks before he dies are in the form of a question. It seems fitting that Jesus, who is so full of questions during his life, would have a question on his lips as he approaches death.

And yet, the question Jesus asks on the cross is different from all of his other questions. It is not a rhetorical question or a teaching tool. It is not offered for the benefit of Jesus' hearers. Rather, it is an agonizing question that is difficult to hear. This question stands alone, which is appropriate because the question is itself an expression of isolation: "My God, my God, why have you forsaken me?" This question is raw and threatening, like an open wound. It sounds like an expression of despair, of hopelessness, of doubt even, which, of course, is just what it is. And it hangs in the air unanswered.

We are never very good at letting those whom we admire be fully human, shed human tears, or express human agony. And when the one we hear expressing despair is Jesus, it is not just our view of him that can be shaken but also our view of God and our view of ourselves. If Jesus doubts, even for a moment, it can seem like enough to scatter our light and fragile faith.

In recent years a number of authors, sometimes dubbed "the New Atheists," have written extensively about their conviction that there is no God because belief in God is "unreasonable" and not consistent with modern science. Their writings have gotten a lot of attention. (The kind of skepticism they represent is nothing new. In the 1920s, the renowned theologian Rudolf Bultmann asked how one can continue to believe in God in the age of the wireless radio.) For most people, however, questions about the existence of God are not the result of intellectual inquiry. Instead, such questions arise out of human experience, particularly the experience of suffering or tragedy. It is the age-old question, which can be traced back at least as far as the Old Testament book of Job: why do bad things happen to good people? That question appears in the midst of life. It is life, not theory, that gives rise to doubt. In most instances, the greatest obstacle to faith is not belief's irrationality but life's injustice.

So Jesus' words on the cross are a response to the greatest threat to faith there is—life's injustice and the apparent absence of God. And Jesus does not banish the darkness with a statement of faith. Rather, his response is an anguished question, and an unanswered question, at that.

It is not surprising, then, that Jesus' question from the cross is seldom left to stand in its stark and raw simplicity. Biblical commentators and preachers alike often interpret his question in ways that make it at least somewhat easier to hear.

We are reminded by some that Jesus' question, "My God,

my God, why have you forsaken me?" are the first words of Psalm 22, a psalm of lament. Lament is a genre that is generously represented in the Bible; in fact, one third of the psalms are psalms of lament. There is also an entire book of the Bible devoted to lament. It is the Old Testament book appropriately entitled Lamentations. In fact, there are more prayers of lament in the Bible than there are prayers of praise.

Laments follow a particular pattern that is reflected in Psalm 22. First, a lament typically begins with an expression of grief and consternation that God does not seem to be doing God's job, usually accompanied by an insistence that God be God. The first verses of the psalm are an example:

> *My God! My God,*
> *why have you forsaken me?*
> *Why are you so far from saving me—*
> *so far from my anguished groans?*
> *My God, I cry out during the day,*
> *but you don't answer;*
> *even at nighttime I don't stop.*
> *(Psalm 22:1-2)*

Then, a lament turns to pleas for God's help:

> *But you, LORD! Don't be far away!*
> *You are my strength!*
> *Come quick and help me!*
> *(Psalm 22:19)*

Finally, a lament ends with an expression of affirmation and trust, often including a reminder of how God has been faithful in the past:

All of you who revere the LORD—praise him!
 All of you who are Jacob's descendants—honor
him!
 All of you who are all Israel's offspring—
  stand in awe of him!
Because he didn't despise or detest
 the suffering of the one who suffered—
 he didn't hide his face from me.
 No, he listened when I cried out to him for help.
(Psalm 22:23-24)

One might summarize the movements of a lament in this way: First, "God, you are not doing your job." Second, "God, you need to do your job." Third, "I am confident you will do your job because you have in the past."

The point here is that Jesus knew this pattern of lament, as would his hearers. Jesus quotes only the beginning of the psalm, but he also knows how it ends. It begins with a most despairing question, "My God, my God, why have you forsaken me?" but it ends with a great affirmation of faith. And those who hear his anguished question from the cross would also know how the psalm ends. Even if only the agony of the psalm is voiced, the concluding affirmation would be supplied by the mind's ear of the person hearing Jesus. That is one way people have come to terms with Jesus' expression of desolation.

Others have come to terms with the challenge of Jesus' question from the cross in a somewhat different way. They point out that, as despairing as these words sound, they are still words of a believer, even in pain, still directed to God. It is, after all, *"My* God, *my* God" to whom he cries.

Jewish author Elie Wiesel, who as a boy was imprisoned in the concentration camp at Auschwitz, tells a story that reflects some of this same dynamic:

> Inside the kingdom of night I witnessed a strange trial. Three rabbis, all erudite and pious men, decided one winter evening to indict God for having allowed his children to be massacred. An awesome conclave, particularly in view of the fact that it was held in a concentration camp. But what happened next is to me even more awesome still. After the trial at which God had been found guilty as charged, one of the rabbis looked at the watch which he had somehow managed to preserve in the kingdom of night and said, "Ah, it is time for prayers." And with that the three rabbis, all erudite and pious men, all bowed their heads and prayed.[12]

Perhaps the words of the persecuted Jesus may be viewed in the same way. The God who has been found guilty of absence remains a God to be approached through prayer. The God who is absent is still *"My God, my God."* In moments of agony that is sometimes the closest we can come to a statement of faith.

These interpretations of Jesus' words of agony can be appropriate, even helpful if they set a context in which we can better understand Jesus' words. They are not helpful, however, if we let such interpretations take the stinging edge off Jesus' words, which somehow manage to stand as powerful as ever anyway, beyond our ability to mute or diminish. Besides, as difficult as it may be to let these words stand as stark and threatening as they sound, it is only when we do so that we can receive their true blessing.

So let us assume that Jesus actually felt forsaken, that what we read and hear from Jesus is true despair, a true sense of being forsaken. The hour was dark, we are told, and in more ways than one. It was dark, with the kind of eerie darkness that can fall like a pall over the world in midday. And it is a dark time for Jesus, what has been called the dark night of the soul, which can lengthen ominous shadows at any time of day. Although death is the greatest isolator of all, it is clear that Jesus is not here expressing the fear of death. Rather, as he faces death, what prompts his cry is the sense of being forsaken by all who loved him, even forsaken by God.

"Misery loves company," or so the old adage has it. But abject misery is isolating as nothing else this side of death has the power to be. Abject misery does not seek company; it knows no company. A cry of misery can have no accompaniment. Into the most important areas of life we go single file. We are born single file. We die single file. We enter life's darkest days single file, face our greatest disappointments single file, without companions, and necessarily so. Where we go in those moments, no one else can follow. And those are lonely

◆◆◆◆◆◆◆◆◆

No one feels so alone as the one who feels deserted by God. And note the cruel irony that the absence of God is only a problem for the believer.

moments, with a kind of loneliness that cannot be quenched, because there is no companion anywhere to be found who can share them.

But, certainly, God is the exception. We are never forsaken by God. God can accompany us into the dark times, the despairing, dark times. And yet, even if God is not absent, God may be perceived as absent, which is just as agonizing. "My God, my God, why have you forsaken me?" It is the question of those who wonder how it is that circumstances seem to conspire against them and who begin to conclude that God is in on the conspiracy. It is the question of the patient who clutches the sheets of his hospital bed, the question of the prisoner in Auschwitz who watches a grim parade of family and friends being led to the their deaths, and the question of any who, out of their misery, cry with the poet Samuel Taylor Coleridge, "Alone, alone, all, all alone, alone on a wide wide sea." And it is Jesus' question.

No one feels so alone as the one who feels deserted by God. And note the cruel irony that the absence of God is only a problem for the believer. Furthermore, the greater one's faith, the greater the potential for disillusionment when that faith is directed toward a God who seems to have left without a trace. It is the one who rejoices most in God's presence who is the most bereft when God is gone. By this measure, could anyone have felt so deserted, so alone, all, all alone, as Jesus on the cross?

"My God, my God, why have you forsaken me?" It is difficult to let that question stand, raw and not explained away, yet there are gracious benefits in doing just that. A Jesus who would experience the full range of human circumstances and human emotions must surely experience the sense of being forsaken. He came to live among us, not as God in a human costume that can be shed whenever things begin to get hard and rough. But, rather, in Jesus, God came as human to the bone, which means human enough to experience human doubts, bone-deep despair, and even the perceived absence of God. If Jesus never experiences these things, that would mean that he never experiences the kind of human life that we live, which is filled with such things.

To be sure, I have never experienced the kind of suffering Jesus endured on the cross, but you do not have to experience pain on that scale to ask God, "Why have you forsaken me?" Life being what it is, at one time or another, in one form or another, everyone has occasion to ask that question. What Jesus' question on the cross says to me is that even my feelings of being abandoned by God are not foreign to God. Even in my abandonment, I am still known by God. My question of God's absence is God's own question, and to ask it is—curiously, mysteriously—to participate in the shape of God's own questioning life.

The Apostle's Creed contains this affirmation about Jesus: "Jesus Christ was crucified, dead and buried. He descended to hell." The last part of that statement always used to trouble me, until one day someone told me that, for her, it is the most treasured part of the creed. When I asked why, she answered, "Because hell is where I spend much of my life." Hell—the dark night of the soul, a sense of being forsaken, the absence of God, a place of despair. We have been there. And Jesus has been there. In fact, he has been with us. And having been there, Jesus transforms it. He transforms the experience of any and all who have been in hell, transforms it by his presence, which cannot help but transform even the darkest regions.

One who would rescue those trapped in a mine shaft sometimes must enter into the danger and darkness of that place himself. How else can those who are trapped be saved, if the one who knows the way out is not willing to be trapped with them?

Before a savior can share his light with us, he must first enter into our darkness, including the darkness of agony and despair. The story of Jesus despairing on the cross is the story of a God willing to experience our hopelessness, that we might have hope, and the story of a God willing to share in human defeat, that we might, in turn, share God's victory.

For that reason, this despairing question that we find difficult to hear may end up being the most important—and ultimately, the most hopeful—question Jesus ever asked.

CHAPTER 12

QUESTIONS FROM
THE RISEN CHRIST

❖❖❖❖❖❖❖❖❖

IF EVER THERE WERE A TIME WHEN YOU MIGHT expect Jesus to
stick with simple declarative sentences, it would be after his
resurrection. While Jesus was alive he could use questions to
provoke or teach. But after his resurrection? Certainly something else is called for then. Perhaps a simple declaration:
"I'm back." Or something theological: "I came back to show
you that sin and death cannot defeat me." Or something reassuring: "I love you and I always will." Or something whimsical: "Hey, you're not going to believe this..."

To be sure, the risen Jesus does offer his followers a few
statements that are quite direct—such as, "Peace be with
you," and "I myself will be with you every day until the end of
this present age."

What is more striking, however, is that even when Jesus
appears to his disciples after his death, he is still asking questions. I think that's because asking questions is so central to

his life and teachings that they could not be abandoned even now. If Jesus did not ask questions after his resurrection, then he would be a different Jesus from the one who walked the earth. Besides, how could his followers be expected to know for sure that it is really Jesus unless he is still asking questions?

And if Jesus is going to ask questions on such a momentous day, you might expect he would have commensurately momentous questions to ask—probing questions, provocative questions. But some of the questions he asks after his resurrection are oddly commonplace. On this day of days, he asks everyday questions.

After the crucifixion, two of Jesus' followers are walking away from Jerusalem on the road to Emmaus. When Jesus gets near the two, he simply asks them what they are talking about, a kind of matter-of-fact question you would ask good friends. It is the kind of question a boy might ask, out of breath, as he catches up with two friends walking home from school: "Say, what's up? What are you talking about?"

In another account, the risen Jesus stands on the beach watching some of his disciples fishing from a boat. He asks, "Have you caught anything to eat?" It is a question fishermen are used to hearing, particularly from those who have no experience with fishing. No fisherman I know would ask the question that way. It's just not done. Phrasing the question that way implies that success is up to the fisherman, which is particularly annoying when the answer is no, as it is in this case. So the preferred way to ask that question among fishermen is, "Any luck?" But Jesus is a landlubber. How is he expected to know that?

One question asked by the risen Jesus sounds just as mundane, but it is one of those questions that, upon further reflection, has far-reaching implications. According to Luke, soon after Jesus appears to his disciples, he asks, "Do you have anything to eat?"

That doesn't sound like the question of a risen Lord. It sounds more like the question of a teenager arriving home from school: "Hey, I'm starving. What's there to eat?"

Jesus' disciples respond to his question in the only suitable way: they give him something to eat, a broiled fish, and he eats it.

In a way, it's a hilarious scene. Apparently, this rising from the dead business really works up an appetite. Who knew? Get this fellow something to eat!

But there's more to it. Eating in front of his disciples is a way to demonstrate that he is real. He isn't a ghost. Ghosts don't eat. It's a way of making clear that Jesus isn't a figment of his disciples' imaginations. The resurrection is not merely a psychological experience in the minds of his followers. It is Jesus, in the midst of them again, in a way that was previously unknown and as unimaginable to them as it is to us.

Some years ago I read a book about children's views of God. The author interviewed dozens of English schoolchildren. As I recall, one child said something like, "I think God floats behind a cloud to eat sausages sometimes." That is a charming English schoolchild way of saying that God is real. If you "eat sausages sometimes," you are real. And I think Luke is saying much the same thing by describing Jesus eating broiled fish. He's real.

In the case of Jesus, however, it means something more. It is a way of reaffirming that Jesus, even the resurrected Jesus, is not some divine being who is distant from human experience. After all, he can experience hunger. Even in his glorified state, he knows the very human experience of being hungry. Heard this way, the question, "Do you have anything to eat?" shows vulnerability. Picture the question on a makeshift cardboard sign, held by a homeless man bundled against the cold. It is a plea born of vulnerability: "Do you have anything to eat?" The scriptural observation that "man does not live on bread alone" is undeniably true. But it is just as true that no one lives very long without it either. Jesus' need for food, even after he is raised, is a reminder that he still remains vulnerable.

And notice what kind of food he is served. You or I may not eat broiled fish all that often, but Jesus ate it all the time—particularly since he hung out with fishermen. So, for him, broiled fish is the kind of comfort food associated with home. When our adult children come home after a time away, I often make fettuccini with my famous Bolognese sauce (OK, famous in our household) for just that reason. The aroma, the taste, the way it looks on the plate, the memory of all the times we have eaten it together—every familiar dimension of the experience evokes home and homecoming. Food can do that. For my children, it is fettuccini with Bolognese sauce. For Jesus, it is broiled fish.

All of this talk about Jesus eating might lead you to a common misconception about the resurrection as it is described in the Gospels. The Gospel writers do not describe Jesus after the resurrection as having a resuscitated human body. Their accounts are more textured, more subtle than that.

For instance, in some accounts the risen Jesus suddenly appears and then disappears again, as quickly as a thought. You might even conclude from those verses that Jesus is a spiritual presence, more than a physical one—whatever that might look like.

But then, at other points—as when Jesus asks, "Do you have anything to eat?"—it sounds like he appears in bodily form. Affirming both, somehow at the same time, is a way for the Gospel writers to point to the mystery of what they proclaim. It is a way of presenting the striking truth to us who were not there to be struck by the experience: He lives!—as surely as you or I live, yet in a different way all the same.

After all, the Gospel writers are trying to describe a reality that finally is indescribable, like trying to describe spring to those who have only known winter, or life itself to those who have never lived.

So the language is not so much descriptive as it is evocative, chosen to evoke in us the same reaction that was surely theirs. It is as if the disciples and Gospel writers are trying to describe music to those who are deaf—so they dance and hope we catch a small sense of what music is about, for a small sense is enough. It is as if they are trying to describe a sunset to those who are blind—so they say it is like a trumpet fanfare and hope

> ✦✦✦✦✦✦✦✦
>
> The Gospel writers are trying to describe a reality that finally is indescribable, like trying to describe spring to those who have only known winter, or life itself to those who have never lived.

we catch a glimmer of the majesty and power of it, for a glimmer is still enough.

Jesus' question, "Do you have anything to eat?" also points his disciples back to the promise he had made just a few days earlier. On that Thursday night, when Jesus gathered with his friends and disciples, he said, "I will be with you every time you gather at table." He wanted to give them something to do in remembrance. And what he chose was a simple meal, something his disciples had shared many times and would share many times after Jesus is gone. By choosing such an everyday event, Jesus was reminding them that he would be with them throughout their days, even the most mundane of Thursdays, through the most simple and common of activities.

Of course, since that time we have made a sacrament of it. We call it Communion or the Eucharist. It's something we do at church. And, of course, that is all fitting. But when Jesus first spoke the words, "Do this in remembrance of me," he was not referring to a sacrament. He was referring to a common meal. He was saying, in essence, "Every time you break bread together, I'll be there."

These days, people sometimes talk about their "spiritual lives" or their "spirituality." But when Jesus asks, "Do you have anything to eat?" it is a reminder that Jesus is not interested in our spiritual lives. He is interested in our whole lives, the lives we actually live. Jesus refuses to be confined to what we describe as "spiritual." He is interested in the day-to-day living of our lives and shows up in the midst of the most common of human activities—like catching up with friends, as he did on the road to Emmaus, or like eating a broiled fish dinner.

In his Gospel, John also writes about the risen Jesus eating broiled fish, but in his story Jesus is the chef. While the disciples are out fishing, Jesus builds a fire. When they come ashore, Jesus is already broiling some fish. This time it is Jesus who invites his disciples to dig into some comfort food. He says, "Come and have breakfast."

So the disciples sit and eat. When breakfast is almost over, Jesus turns to Peter and addresses him, "Simon son of John..." It is Peter's full name, the form of his name that Jesus only uses when he really means business. Then comes the question—and it is a question that sounds quite different from the inquiry about breakfast—"Do you love me more than these others do?"

Is there any more vulnerable question than this?

Jesus' question, "Do you have anything to eat?" is a question that reflects physical vulnerability. We all need food to survive, and apparently even the risen Jesus does as well. The question, "Do you love me?" reveals a different kind of vulnerability—an emotional vulnerability—because we all want to be loved, and apparently even the risen Jesus does as well.

In a way, it is disquieting to hear this question from Jesus. It seems like an unwelcome role reversal. After all, isn't it Jesus' job to love us? In spite of our stumbling and our bumbling, even in the face of our fickle faith, Jesus is supposed to love us. Isn't that the essence of the good news? "For God so loved the world that he gave his only Son."

When Jesus asks to be loved, it suggests a vulnerability that I'm not sure I want Jesus to have. It does not make Jesus sound emotionally needy, exactly, but it does imply that he has emotional needs. To suggest that Jesus might want love suggests that he might be very much like you or me, because we all want to be loved. Which, of course, is just the point. Jesus is like us, vulnerable to the hurts of life, even now, after he is raised.

When Jesus asks Peter, "Do you love me more than these?" he immediately responds: "Yes, Lord, you know I love you." And Jesus says, "Feed my lambs."

Jesus asks the question a second time: "Simon son of John, do you love me?" And Peter's response is the same: "Yes, Lord, you know I love you." Jesus says, "Take care of my sheep."

But Jesus just won't let this question go. He asks it yet a third time: "Simon son of John, do you love me?" By this time, Peter's feelings are hurt. He thinks that Jesus asks the question numerous times because he doubts Peter's devotion, and that bugs Peter. It is not hard to hear the irritation in his voice as he elaborates on his answer: "Lord, you know everything; you know I love you." Jesus says, "Feed my sheep."

It is one of the only questions Jesus repeats. But why does he repeat it three times?

After Jesus was arrested, Peter is among those huddled around a fire in the courtyard of the Temple. Three times Peter is asked if he knows Jesus, and three times he denies any association with him. So perhaps Jesus asks Peter for three expressions of love to give him a chance to redeem his three denials. There would at least be some symmetry to that.

But there may be another reason Jesus repeats this question. In Greek, the original language of the New Testament, there is more than one word to describe love. One word is *agape*, which is unconditional love, the love that does not ask for anything in return, self-giving love, sacrificial love. It is the kind of love associated with Jesus. Followers of Jesus aim to reflect this kind of love in their interactions with one another, but as limited creatures, we seldom reflect true *agape* in our relationships.

Another word in Greek that is translated as love is *phileo*, which is brotherly or sisterly love. It is the kind of love associated with friendships—warm and generous but not completely unconditional. This form of love is more within our grasp.

This distinction is important to understanding the exchange between Jesus and Peter.

The first two times Jesus asks Peter, "Do you love me?" he is using the word *agape*. And both times when Peter responds, "Yes, Lord, you know I love you," he is using the word *phileo*. In other words, Jesus asks Peter if he loves him with the kind of unconditional love associated with *agape*, but Peter is not able to respond in those terms. Peter may not be capable of *agape* yet, but he is able to love Jesus like a brother, like a true friend.

Recognizing Peter's limitations, Jesus asks the question a third time, but in a different way. The third time, when Jesus asks, "Do you love me?" he is using the word *phileo*. And this time, Peter is able to respond in kind: "Yes, Lord, you know I love (*phileo*) you." In other words, the third time around, Jesus asks the question at Peter's level. Peter may not yet be capable of *agape*, of unconditional love, but he is capable of *phileo*, of loving Jesus like a brother and friend. So that is what Jesus

✦✦✦✦✦✦✦✦✦

If you want to grasp
what a Christian life
entails, repeat often
these three questions
and hold them close.

asks of him. The third time Jesus asks the question, he asks Peter for love in full measure, but for the kind of love of which he is capable.

There are three questions that Jesus repeats in the Gospels. Those three questions, read together, capture so much about what it means to encounter Jesus:

Jesus asks, "What are you looking for?"

He asks, "What do you want me to do for you?"

And he asks, "Do you love me?"

"What are you looking for?" is a question for those who yearn for God knows what (quite literally) and end up concluding that what they are yearning for is God.

"What do you want me to do for you?" is the question asked by a Lord who acts more like a servant, eager to tend to our needs.

"Do you love me?" is the question asked by someone who wants to be in relationship with you and is willing to become completely vulnerable in order to do so.

If you want to grasp what a Christian life entails, repeat often these three questions and hold them close.

CHAPTER 13

ALL THOSE QUESTIONS

✦✦✦✦✦✦✦✦✦

THE CHURCH WHERE I WAS PASTOR FOR TWENTY years once studied the questions Jesus asks in small groups. In preparation for those gatherings, I compiled a list of about 150 of the questions Jesus asks. With each of the small groups we began by taking turns reading all 150 questions around the circle—without commentary, without context, without citation. Just the questions. Some of the questions were as familiar as our own names, and other questions felt like we were hearing them for the first time. Even those of us who were familiar with the questions were used to reading them embedded in the text. The experience of hearing one question after another—a shower of questions, a tide of questions—helped us hear them anew in a way that was powerful. It was as if spending time with the questions, so central to Jesus' ministry, was a way to spend time with Jesus, and we wanted to linger there for a time.

Not all of the questions are easy to hear, however. Jesus' questions have the power both to comfort and to challenge. You may find that you want to linger with some questions and turn away from others. That is to be expected. Questions can be very powerful, even threatening. Socrates was killed for asking questions. And, in a sense, Jesus was, also.

Many people spend their entire lives seeking answers, when it can be more important to find the right questions. What Albert Einstein said in a different context is just as true here: "If I had an hour to solve a problem and my life depended on the solution, I would spend the first 55 minutes determining the proper question to ask, for once I know the proper question, I could solve the problem in less than five minutes."

Indeed, sometimes our lives depend on finding the right question, and that is certainly the case in the life of faith. After all, there is no such thing as a right answer to the wrong question.

Whatever else it might mean to follow Jesus, certainly it means letting Jesus' questions guide our lives, rather than our own questions. Following Jesus is living the questions that Jesus asks.

✦✦✦✦✦✦✦✦✦

Whatever else it might mean to follow Jesus, certainly it means letting Jesus' questions guide our lives, rather than our own questions. Following Jesus is living the questions that Jesus asks.

In the pages that follow, there is a compilation of Jesus' questions. We found at our church that it is most effective to read the questions aloud—without commentary, context, or citation—preferably in a group.

After you have finished your reading, don't immediately reach for a Bible to see the context of a question. Let the question remain for a time in the context of the moment. Pause to consider which question seemed to jump out at you. You don't have to know why.

Here are some additional questions for your reflection on the experience of reading the questions Jesus asks:

Which question do you find most comforting? Is there also something challenging about that same question?

Which question do you find most challenging? Is there also something comforting about that same question?

Is there a question you find yourself running toward?

Is there a question you find yourself wanting to run away from?

Is there a question you would want to take with you throughout the next week?

Is there a question you would want Jesus to ask of you at the end of your life?

Is there a question you wish Jesus had asked that he didn't ask?

Is there a question you wish Jesus hadn't asked?

What question occupies or preoccupies you in your own life that is not among the questions Jesus asks?

If you could substitute one of Jesus' questions for the question that occupies or preoccupies you in your own life, would you? If so, which of Jesus' questions would you choose?

This book concludes with the questions Jesus asks. It is fitting that Jesus has the last word and also fitting that the last word is a question.

Invitation

What are you looking for? (John 1:38)

Who are you looking for? (John 18:7 and 20:15)

Why were you looking for me? (Luke 2:49)

What do you want? (Matthew 20:21)

What do you want me to do for you? (Matthew 20:32; Mark 10:36 and 10:51; Luke 18:41)

Identity

Who do people say that I am? (Mark 8:27; Luke 9:18; Matthew 16:13)

But who do you say that I am? (Mark 8:29; Luke 9:20; Matthew 16:15)

Why do you ask me about what is good? (Matthew 19:17)

Why do you call me good? (Mark 10:18; Luke 18:19)

Woman, what does that have to do with me? (John 2:4)

Who is my mother? Who are my brothers? (Matthew 12:48; Mark 3:33)

What do you think about the Christ? Whose son is he? (Matthew 22:42)

The wedding guests can't fast while the groom is with them, can they? (Mark 2:19; Luke 5:34)

The wedding guests can't mourn while the groom is still with them, can they? (Matthew 9:15)

Man, who appointed me as judge or referee between you and your brother? (Luke 12:14)

You faithless generation, how long will I be with you? How long will I put up with you? (Mark 9:19; Luke 9:41; Matthew 17:17)

Lord, when was it that we saw you hungry and gave you food, or thirsty and gave you something to drink? And when was it that we saw you a stranger and welcomed you, or naked and gave you clothing? And when was it that we saw you sick or in prison and visited you? ... Lord, when was it that we saw you hungry or thirsty or a stranger or naked or sick or in prison, and did not take care of you? (Matthew 25:37-39, 44)

Don't you know me, Philip, even after I have been with you all this time? Whoever has seen me has seen the Father. How can you say, "Show us the Father"? (John 14:9)

Purity of Heart

Why do you raise such questions in your hearts? (Luke 5:22)

Why do think evil in your hearts? (Matthew 9:4)

Didn't the one who made the outside also make the inside? (Luke 11:40)

Conversion

Why do you see the splinter that's in your brother's or sister's eye, but don't notice the log in your own eye? How can you say to your brother or sister, "Let me take the splinter out of your eye," when there's a log in your eye? (Matthew 7:3-4; Luke 6:41-42)

Do you think the suffering of these Galileans proves that they were more sinful than all the other Galileans? What about those twelve people who were killed when the tower of Siloam fell on them? Do you think that they were more guilty of wrongdoing than everyone else who lives in Jerusalem? (Luke 13:2, 4)

Love

If you love only those who love you, what reward do you have? Don't even the tax collectors do the same? (Matthew 5:46; Luke 6:32)

And if you greet only your brothers and sisters, what more are you doing? (Matthew 5:47)

If you do good to those who do good to you, what credit is that to you? ... If you lend to those from whom you hope to receive, what credit is that to you? (Luke 6:33-34)

Which of them will love him more? (Luke 7:42)

Healing

Do you want to get well? (John 5:6)

Who touched me? (Luke 8:45; Mark 5:30)

What is your name? (Mark 5:9; Luke 8:30)

How long has this been going on? (Mark 9:21)

Which is easier—to say to a paralyzed person, "Your sins are forgiven," or to say, "Get up, take up your bed, and walk"? (Mark 2:9; Matthew 9:5; Luke 5:23)

What do you want me to do for you? (Matthew 20:32; Mark 10:51; Luke 18:41)

Vision

Do you see anything? (Mark 8:23)

Do you see all these things? (Matthew 24:2)

A blind person can't lead another blind person, right? Won't they both fall into a ditch? (Luke 6:39)

Do you see this woman? (Luke 7:44)

What if you were to see the Son of Man ascending to where he was before? (John 6:62)

Compassion

What do you think? Which one of these three was a neighbor to the man who encountered thieves? (Luke 10:36)

Woman, where are they? Is there no one to condemn you? (John 8:10)

Why do you make trouble for her? (Mark 14:6; Matthew 26:10)

The Meaning of Life

Why would people gain the whole world but lose their lives? (Mark 8:36; Luke 9:25; Matthew 16:26)

What will people give in exchange for their lives? (Mark 8:37)

Can any of you by worrying add a single hour to your span of life? If then you are not able to do so small a thing as that, why do you worry about the rest? (Matthew 6:27; Luke 12:26)

Is not life more than food and the body more than clothing? (Matthew 6:25)

Are you not of more value than [the birds of the air]? (Matthew 6:26)

Is it legal on the Sabbath to do good or to do evil, to save life or to destroy it? (Luke 6:9; Mark 3:4)

So which one is greater, the one who is seated at the table or the one who serves at the table? Isn't it the one who is seated at the table? (Luke 22:27)

The Reign of God

What is God's kingdom like? To what can I compare it? (Luke 13:18)

What's a good image for God's kingdom? What parable can I use to explain it? (Mark 4:30)

Do you think that I have come to bring peace to the earth? (Luke 12:51)

God's Generosity

Why do you worry about clothing? (Matthew 6:28)

Who among you will give your children a stone when they ask for bread? Or give them a snake when they ask for fish? (Matthew 7:9-10)

Which father among you would give a snake to your child if the child asked for a fish? If a child asked for an egg, what father would give the child a scorpion? If you who are evil know how to give good gifts to your children, how much more will the heavenly Father give the Holy Spirit to those who ask him? (Luke 11:11-13)

How much bread do you have? (Matthew 15:34; Mark 6:38, 8:5)

If God so clothes the grass of the field, which is alive today and tomorrow is thrown into the oven, will he not much more clothe you—you of little faith? (Matthew 6:30; Luke 12:28)

Won't God provide justice to his chosen people who cry out to him day and night? Will he be slow to help them? (Luke 18:7)

Weren't ten cleansed? Where are the other nine? (Luke 17:17-18)

Faith

Where is your faith? (Luke 8:25)

Do you believe in the Son of Man? (John 9:35)

Do you believe I can do this? (Matthew 9:28)

You of little faith, why did you doubt? (Matthew 14:31)

Why are you afraid? Have you still no faith? (Mark 4:40)

When the Son of Man comes, will he find faith on earth? (Luke 18:8)

If you don't believe the writings of Moses, how will you believe my words? (John 5:47)

What's all this commotion and crying about? (Mark 5:39)

Why does this generation look for a sign? (Mark 8:12)

To what will I compare the people of this generation? What are they like? (Luke 7:31; Matthew 11:16)

How can you believe when you receive praise from each other but don't seek the praise that comes from the only God? (John 5:44)

Didn't I tell you that if you believe, you will see God's glory? (John 11:40)

Don't you believe that I am in the Father and the Father is in me? (John 14:10)

Do you now believe? (John 16:31)

Truth

Who among you can show I'm guilty of sin? Since I speak the truth, why don't you believe me? (John 8:46)

Does the Law allow healing on the Sabbath or not? (Luke 14:3)

Was John's baptism of heavenly or of human origin? (Luke 20:4; Mark 11:30)

Show me a coin. Whose image and inscription does it have on it? (Luke 20:24; Mark 12:16; Matthew 22:20)

Understanding

Why don't you understand what I'm saying? (John 8:43)

Why are you talking about the fact that you don't have any bread? Don't you grasp what has happened? Don't you understand? Are your hearts so resistant to what God is doing? Don't you have eyes? Why can't you see? Don't you have ears? Why can't you hear? Don't you remember? (Mark 8:17-18)

You are a teacher of Israel and you don't know these things? (John 3:10)

If I have told you about earthly things and you don't believe, how will you believe if I tell you about heavenly things? (John 3:12)

Don't you understand either? (Mark 7:18)

Have you understood all these things? (Matthew 13:51)

How is it that you don't know how to interpret the present time? (Luke 12:56)

And why don't you judge for yourselves what is right? (Luke 12:57)

Isn't this the reason you are wrong, because you don't know either the scriptures or God's power? (Mark 12:24)

Does this offend you? (John 6:61)

Obedience

Why do you call me "Lord, Lord," and don't do what I say? (Luke 6:46)

Why do you break the command of God by keeping the rules handed down to you? (Matthew 15:3)

What were you arguing about during the journey? (Mark 9:33)

Who are the faithful and wise managers whom the master will put in charge of his household servants, to give them their food at the proper time? (Luke 12:42)

Why are you testing me? (Mark 12:15; Matthew 22:18)

Hasn't it been written, "My house will be called a house of prayer for all nations?" (Mark 11:17)

Discipleship

Will you give up your life for me? (John 13:38)

Can you drink from the cup that I'm about to drink from? (Matthew 20:22; Mark 10:38)

Do you also want to leave? (John 6:67)

Didn't I choose you twelve? (John 6:70)

When I sent you out without a wallet, bag, or sandals, you didn't lack anything, did you? (Luke 22:35)

Do you know what I've done for you? (John 13:12)

My Father's house has room to spare. If that weren't the case, would I have told you that I'm going to prepare a place for you? (John 14:2)

Could you not keep awake one hour? (Mark 14:37; Matthew 26:40)

Will you sleep and rest all night? (Mark 14:41; Matthew 26:45)

Why are you sleeping? (Luke 22:46)

Arrest and Trial

Who are you looking for? (John 18:4, 7)

Am I not to drink the cup the Father has given me? (John 18:11)

Judas, is it with a kiss that you are betraying the Son of Man? (Luke 22:48)

Have you come with swords and clubs to arrest me, as though I were a thief? (Mark 14:48; Luke 22:52; Matthew 26:55)

Or do you think that I'm not able to ask my Father and he will send to me more than twelve battle groups of angels right away? But if I did that, how would the scriptures be fulfilled that say this must happen? (Matthew 26:53-54)

Why ask me? (John 18:21)

If I speak wrongly, testify about what was wrong. But if I speak correctly, why do you strike me? (John 18:23)

Do you say this on your own or have others spoken to you about me? (John 18:34)

The Cross

Why do you want to kill me? (John 7:19)

For which of those works do you stone me? (John 10:32)

What should I say? "Father, save me from this time"? (John 12:27)

My God, my God, why have you left me? (Mark 15:34; Matthew 27:46)

The Resurrection

Woman, why are you crying? Who are you looking for? (John 20:15)

As for the resurrection of the dead, haven't you read what God told you, "I'm the God of Abraham, the God of Isaac, and the God of Jacob?" He isn't the God of the dead but of the living. (Matthew 22:31-32)

Everyone who lives and believes in me will never die. Do you believe this? (John 11:26)

What are you talking about as you walk along? What things? (Luke 24:17, 19)

Wasn't it necessary for the Christ to suffer these things and then enter into his glory? (Luke 24:26)

Why are you startled? Why are doubts arising in your hearts? (Luke 24:38)

Do you have anything to eat? (Luke 24:41)

Do you believe because you see me? (John 20:29)

Children, have you caught anything to eat? (John 21:5)

Simon, son of John, do you love me more than these? ... Do you love me? ... Do you love me? (John 21:15-17)[13]

NOTES

1. John Dear, *The Questions of Jesus* (New York: Doubleday, 2004), xxii; Eric Burtness, *Lenten Journey: Beyond Question* (Minneapolis: Augsburg Fortress, 2012), 9.

2. Dear, *The Questions of Jesus,* xxii.

3. Rainer Maria Rilke, *Letters to a Young Poet* (New York: Random House, 1986), 34.

4. Wayne Cordeiro, *Doing Church as a Team* (Ventura, CA: Regal Books, 2001), 32–33.

5. Parker J. Palmer, *Let Your Life Speak* (San Francisco: Jossey-Bass, 2000), 44–46.

6. Robin Pogrebin, "Loved, but Abandoned and Sold," *New York Times,* July 23, 1999.

7. Frederick Buechner, *Wishful Thinking: A Theological ABC* (New York, Hagerstown, San Francisco, London: Harper & Row, 1973), 12.

8. Ibid., 12.

9. Ibid., 12.

10. Walter Brueggemann, "The Liturgy of Abundance, the Myth of Scarcity," *The Christian Century* (March 24-31, 1999), 24.

11. C. S. Lewis, *Mere Christianity* (New York: Macmillan, 1960), 55–56.

12. Robert McAfee Brown, *Elie Wiesel: Messenger to All Humanity* (Notre Dame: University of Notre Dame Press, 1983), 154.

13. I am indebted to John Dear for the formatting of these questions. See Dear, *The Questions of Jesus,* xi–xix.

READERS GUIDE FOR
JESUS IS THE QUESTION

Introduction: So Many Questions

Martin B. Copenhaver writes that even after thirty-three years of ordained ministry and a lifetime as a Christian, he continues "to learn new things from Jesus and about him." Are you learning new things from and about Jesus? What have you learned from or about him most recently? What is the difference between learning *about* Jesus and learning *from* Jesus?

Were you surprised that Jesus asks so many questions—many more than he is asked, and many more than he answered? What do you make of Jesus' asking all these questions?

Martin recounts telling two friends about how Jesus asks so many questions. One friend said, "I love the idea that Jesus has so many questions, because so do I. That's a comfort." The other friend said, "Funny, that Jesus asks a lot of questions does not sound comforting to me. It sounds decidedly disquieting because I assume Jesus will use questions to challenge me." Do you identify with either or both of these friends? Why or why not?

What do you make of Martin's suggestion that Jesus *is* the question?

Chapter 1
Questions About Longing

Ask yourself, What am I looking for?

Truly sit with the question. Don't bat it away: What am I looking for?

Is this an easy question to answer? a scary question? Why?

Ask people close to you—your spouse, your best friend, your closest coworker—what they think you are looking for. Do their answers please you? surprise you? upset you?

Is there a gap between what you in fact spend your hours and days looking for and what you wish you were looking for? What interferes with your search for those things you most wish you were looking for?

Chapter 2
A Question About Compassion

When have you felt that you want to be seen, but are not?

When have you felt that you did not wish to be seen—but you could not adequately hide?

Martin's friend George says, "May we all see as Jesus sees." What does that mean? How does Jesus see, and how is it different from how the rest of us see most of the time?

Whom have you seen as Jesus sees? What difference did that seeing make in the life of the person seen? What difference did it make in your own life to see so clearly, so fully?

When have you been seen as Jesus sees? By whom? Who do you wish would more fully see you as Jesus sees? What difference would it make in your life to be seen more fully by that person (or by those people)?

Martin lingers over the question of whether he sees himself clearly, truly. Do you really see yourself? Why or why not? What might help you see yourself more as Jesus sees you?

Chapter 3
A Question About Identity

What does it mean to you that Jesus is interested in knowing the names of the people he heals?

Here is the story of Legion, according to Mark (5:1-9):

> Jesus and his disciples came to the other side of the lake, to the region of the Gerasenes. As soon as Jesus got out of the boat, a man possessed by an evil spirit came out of the tombs. This man lived among the tombs, and no one was ever strong enough to restrain him, even with a chain. He had been secured many times with leg irons and chains, but he broke the chains and smashed the leg irons. No one was tough enough to control him. Night and day in the tombs and the hills, he would howl and cut himself with stones. When he saw Jesus from far away, he ran and knelt before him, shouting, "What have you to do with me, Jesus, Son of the Most High God? Swear to God that you won't torture me!" He said this because Jesus had already commanded him, "Unclean spirit, come out of the man!" Jesus asked him, "What is your name?" He responded, "Legion is my name, because we are many."

Reread the story—once, twice more—and imagine yourself as the stricken man whom Jesus heals. Feel Jesus healing you. Then hear Jesus asking your name. What do you say when he asks? What difference does it make to be known by Jesus *by name*?

Chapter 4
Questions About Faith and Doubt

Martin observes that Jesus is not very sympathetic to his disciples' terror: "Why are you afraid? Have you still no faith?" What storms in your life have tested *your* faith? How does it feel to imagine, in those tests, hearing Jesus say to you not, "Don't worry; I understand why you might feel scared and doubtful right about now," but instead, "Why are you afraid? Have you no faith?"

Why do you think Jesus was so impatient with his disciples' doubt?

Chapter 5
Questions About Worry

Martin tells a story about Martin Luther: "On one occasion, when Martin Luther was consumed with worry, his wife began to wear black. When Luther finally asked her why, she replied, 'Haven't you heard? God is dead.'" What is your reaction to this story?

What most worries you? Is it something personal—something specific to your life? (Are you waiting for the doctor to call back with those test results? Is your child's marriage on the rocks? Is yours? Is your sister drinking too much? Are you?) Or is it perhaps something global, structural, over which you are most concerned? (The economy? The environment?) Hold that worry in your open hand, and then hear Jesus asking you, "Why do you worry? Does not God care for the lilies? If God will take care of the lilies, won't God also care for you?" What do you feel when you hear Jesus' questions? Are they rhetorical questions? Perhaps. If you dared, nonetheless, to reply to Jesus, what would you say?

Chapter 6
Questions About the Reach of Love

Martin writes in this chapter about "the reach of love."
How far does your love reach?

Can you recall a moment in your life when your love
reached further than you could have imagined it could
reach? Can you recall a moment when it reached past all the
people who love you, to someone who decidedly does not
love you?

Can you recall a moment in your life when your love did
not reach as far as you now (or even then) wish it had? Is
there a practice you could put in place in your life to help the
reach of your love grow – so that your love reaches further
next year than it does this year?

Has there been a time in your life when your love has
reached too far? What did you learn from that experience?

Chapter 7
Questions About Healing

Has a doctor or other medical provider ever asked you a question that has truly unsettled you? What did you do in response to that question?

Why do you think Jesus' healing involves Jesus posing questions?

Sit quietly for a few minutes, and then hear Jesus say to you, "What do you want me to do for you?" How might you answer?

Chapter 8
A Question About Abundance

Martin writes about the abundance in his own life, and he admits that, despite all the abundance, he sometimes still focuses on what he perceives as scarcity. Where is there abundance in your life? Where do you perceive scarcity— where do you perceive that you do not have enough? What happens when you hold those scarce things next to Jesus' miracle of loaves and fishes?

Set aside a few minutes and prayerfully ponder the relationships in your life—family, friendships, marital or romantic relationships, neighborly relationships. Holding those relationships in your mind's eye, hear Jesus ask you, "How many loaves do you have?"

Set aside a few minutes and prayerfully ponder your work—that might be a paid job, it might be volunteer work in your community, it might be parenting, it might be gardening or painting or baking or writing. Holding your work in your mind's eye, hear Jesus ask you, "How many loaves do you have?"

Set aside a few minutes and prayerfully ponder your finances. Holding your finances in your mind's eye, hear Jesus ask you, "How many loaves do you have?"

Set aside a few minutes and prayerfully ponder time. You might pray through your calendar for the week. You might consider the weeks when time drags, and the weeks when you wish you had more time. Holding your time in your mind's eye, hear Jesus ask you, "How many loaves do you have?"

Chapter 9
The Questions Jesus Answers

Why do you think Jesus answers the few questions he answers?

Which of Jesus' answers most unsettles you? Which most inspires you? Which do you find boring? Which do you find most perplexing? Which do you find most loving?

If you could ask Jesus one question, knowing he would indeed answer, what would the question be?

Chapter 10
Questions About Who Jesus Is

How do you answer Jesus' question, "Who do you say that I am?"

Martin suggests that there is no one right answer to the question "Who do you say I am?" but "all of the true answers have some real consequences for our lives." What are the consequences for your life of your answer to Jesus' question?

What is your response to the story Martin tells about his final sermon at Burlington's First Congregational Church?

After that sermon, Martin's parishioner asked him a question that now haunts him. Who in your life has asked you a question that still haunts you? What is the question? Why does it haunt you so?

Chapter 11
A Question from the Cross

Martin says that "the question Jesus asks on the cross is different from all of his other questions." How is it different?

When have you most recently offered God a heartfelt lament? Are there situations in the world or in your life that you would like to lament? If something prevents you from freely expressing lament, what is getting in the way? What might allow you to more freely lament?

What does the idea that Jesus indeed felt forsaken and experienced desolation on the cross offer to your spiritual life? How does Jesus' own forsakenness draw you nearer to him?

Chapter 12
Questions from the Risen Christ

What strikes you about the questions the resurrected Jesus asks back-to-back: "Do you have any bread?" and "Do you love me more than these others do?" Does it seem strange that a profound question about love follows a straightforward question about food? How does the second question help interpret the first question?

Why does Jesus ask Peter if Peter loves him more than any of the others do? What would you say to Jesus if Jesus asked this to you?

Martin writes, "There are three questions that Jesus repeats in the Gospels. Those three questions, read together, capture so much about what it means to encounter Jesus: Jesus asks, 'What are you looking for?' He asks, 'What do you want me to do for you?' And he asks, 'Do you love me?'" And then Martin suggests, "If you want to grasp what a Christian life entails, repeat often these three questions and hold them close." How might you hold those questions close? Imagine Jesus asking you those questions each day or each week for the next year or the next five years. How might your friendship with Jesus be different five years from now, if you indeed hold those questions close?

Chapter 13
All Those Questions

Martin writes, "Whatever else it might mean to follow Jesus, certainly it means letting Jesus' questions guide our lives, rather than our own questions. Following Jesus is living the questions that Jesus asks."

What might it mean to you to live the question "What are you looking for?" *(John 1:38)*

What might it mean to you to live the question "Who touched me?" *(Luke 8:45; Mark 5:30)*

What might it mean to you to live the questions "What is God's kingdom like?" and "To what can I compare it?" *(Luke 13:18)*

What might it mean to you to live the question "Do you also want to leave?" *(John 6:67)*

Set aside a few moments and read aloud one of the sets of questions Martin has compiled in this chapter. Read aloud the same section five times in a row. What stirs inside you? What stays with you?

FOR FURTHER READING

Below is a list of books. Some are books "about Jesus." Some are books that revivify other biblical characters (including biblical birds) in refreshing ways. Some are books about reading Scripture. These books represent a range of viewpoints and beliefs across a theological spectrum. But each book offers new ways to ask the important questions.

The Questions of Jesus: Challenging Ourselves to Discover Life's Great Answers by John Dear

Knowing Jesus in Your Life by Carol Anderson with Peter Summers

Knowing Jesus by James Alison

Consider the Birds: A Provocative Guide to Birds of the Bible by Debbie Blue

Power and Passion: Six Characters in Search of Resurrection by Samuel Wells

Jesus: A Pilgrimage by James Martin

The Meaning of Mary Magdalene: Discovering the Woman at the Heart of Christianity by Cynthia Bourgeault

Opening the Bible by Thomas Merton

Simply Jesus: A New Vision of Who He Was, What He Did, and Why He Matters by N. T. Wright

The Dwelling of the Light: Praying with Icons of Christ by Rowan Williams

The Gospel in Solentiname by Ernesto Cardenal

Living Jesus: Learning the Heart of the Gospel by Luke Timothy Johnson

Martin B. Copenhaver is the president of Andover Newton Theological School in Newton Centre, Massachusetts, which is the oldest theological school in the country.

A *magna cum laude* graduate of Dickinson College, Martin received his Master of Divinity from Yale Divinity School and currently serves on the board of advisors of Yale Divinity School. He is an ordained minister in the United Church of Christ and most recently has served as senior minister of Wellesley Congregational Church (United Church of Christ) in Massachusetts.

A member of the Still Speaking Writers' Group, Martin also serves as Editor at Large for *The Christian Century*. He is the author of, among other books, *Living Faith While Holding Doubts* and *To Begin at the Beginning*, as well as coauthor, with Lillian Daniel, of the bestselling book *This Odd and Wondrous Calling*, which has the distinction of being the only book that is an assigned text for classes at both Harvard University and Sing Sing Correctional Facility, a maximum security prison.

Martin's wife, Karen Faulds Copenhaver, is an attorney, with a practice in intellectual property law. They have two children, Alanna and Todd.